THE
PO
IDI
GU

Not So
Fac

THE POCKET IDIOT'S GUIDE TO

Not So Useless Facts

by Dane Sherwood, Sandy Wood, and Kara Kovalchik

ALPHA

A member of Penguin Group (USA) Inc.

ALPHA BOOKS

Published by the Penguin Group

Penguin Group (USA) Inc., 375 Hudson Street, New York, New York 10014, U.S.A.

Penguin Group (Canada), 10 Alcorn Avenue, Toronto, Ontario, Canada M4V 3B2 (a division of Pearson Penguin Canada Inc.)

Penguin Books Ltd, 80 Strand, London WC2R 0RL, England

Penguin Ireland, 25 St Stephen's Green, Dublin 2, Ireland (a division of Penguin Books Ltd)

Penguin Group (Australia), 250 Camberwell Road, Camberwell, Victoria 3124, Australia (a division of Pearson Australia Group Pty Ltd)

Penguin Books India Pvt Ltd, 11 Community Centre, Panchsheel Park, New Delhi—110 017, India

Penguin Group (NZ), cnr Airborne and Rosedale Roads, Albany, Auckland 1310, New Zealand (a division of Pearson New Zealand Ltd)

Penguin Books (South Africa) (Pty) Ltd, 24 Sturdee Avenue, Rosebank, Johannesburg 2196, South Africa

Penguin Books Ltd, Registered Offices: 80 Strand, London WC2R 0RL, England

International Standard Book Number: 1-59257-567-6
Library of Congress Catalog Card Number: 2006929114

08 07 06   8 7 6 5 4 3 2 1

Interpretation of the printing code: The rightmost number of the first series of numbers is the year of the book's printing; the rightmost number of the second series of numbers is the number of the book's printing. For example, a printing code of 06-1 shows that the first printing occurred in 2006.

Printed in the United States of America

Note: This publication contains the opinions and ideas of its authors. It is intended to provide helpful and informative material on the subject matter covered. It is sold with the understanding that the authors and publisher are not engaged in rendering professional services in the book. If the reader requires personal assistance or advice, a competent professional should be consulted.

The authors and publisher specifically disclaim any responsibility for any liability, loss, or risk, personal or otherwise, which is incurred as a consequence, directly or indirectly, of the use and application of any of the contents of this book.

Most Alpha books are available at special quantity discounts for bulk purchases for sales promotions, premiums, fund-raising, or educational use. Special books, or book excerpts, can also be created to fit specific needs.

For details, write: Special Markets, Alpha Books, 375 Hudson Street, New York, NY 10014.

Introduction

Science isn't really sure why we modern humans have such short attention spans. It's been linked to everything from MTV to the hole in the ozone layer. We like our information served in small, bite-sized pieces. So that's what you'll find inside this *Pocket Idiot's Guide™*—a variety of *Not So Useless Facts*, trimmed of fat and neatly arranged in an appetizing presentation. Be forewarned, however: you may suffer from Fact Reflux at the most inappropriate times, and find yourself dazzling your friends, co-workers, or even the bus driver with your newfound knowledge of everything from reptiles to fingernails to redundant abbreviations.

For the first 20 years or so of our lives, we're told that we need to learn and grow and expand our minds. Sadly, the manner in which this is accomplished is by cramming kids into stuffy classrooms with wooden desks and rehashing material from out-of-date books. Schools are more concerned with budgets, test scores, and certifications than they are with truly educating kids.

When we leave school and enter "the real world," most of the knowledge gained in school goes away. What's left in the brain fits in one of three categories:

First, there's the information we *have* to know. This ranges from survival instincts (boiling water can scald you) to the stuff necessary to do our jobs (showing up on time, following instructions, maybe a little math—you know, the basics).

Second, there's the information that just gets stuck in our brains for no apparent reason. Have you ever noticed that you can remember your first phone number, or your locker combination from sixth grade? Some data seems to stay stored in areas where it's easy to recall.

Third—and here's where the book you're holding comes in—there's the information that we find interesting, or ironic, or memorable.

That's what *The Pocket Idiot's Guide™ to Not So Useless Facts* hopes to provide you with more of. It doesn't cover every subject, and you won't learn all you need to know about any individual topic in the book. But when information is put in a way that causes a mental reaction, we tend to remember it. If it's very funny, very odd, or very surprising, the brain seems to put it on the front burner. We hope that the facts inside this book will strike you in this manner.

Always remember: **There is no such thing as useless knowledge!**

Trademarks

All terms mentioned in this book that are known to be or are suspected of being trademarks or service marks have been appropriately capitalized. Alpha Books and Penguin Group (USA) Inc. cannot attest to the accuracy of this information. Use of a term in this book should not be regarded as affecting the validity of any trademark or service mark.

Abbreviations & Acronyms

Not a comprehensive list by any means, but a selection of lesser-known samples.

3M—Minnesota Mining & Manufacturing

BASF—Baden Aniline & Soda Factory

BVD—Bradley, Vorhees, & Day

EPCOT—Experimental Prototype Community Of Tomorrow

ESPN—Entertainment & Sports Programming Network

HP (steak sauce)—Houses of Parliament

JVC—Japan Victor Company

M&M (candies)—Mars & Murrie

MCI—Microwave Communications, Inc.

PAM (cooking spray)—Product of Arthur Meyerhoff

QANTAS—Queensland And Northern Territory Aerial Services

RCA—Radio Corporation of America

STP—Scientifically Treated Petroleum

VHS—Video Home System

WD-40—Water Displacement (40th formula)

ZIP (code)—Zone Improvement Plan

The Academy Awards

Only two men won multiple acting Oscars in the 1990s. The obvious one is Tom Hanks; the not-so-obvious one, Kevin Spacey.

Through 1950, only one Best Picture Oscar winner was filmed in color: 1939's *Gone with the Wind*.

Though it's worth many times as much as a collectible, the actual value of an Oscar statuette is estimated at only $150.

Despite a long and distinguished career, Sean Connery has only ever been nominated for a single Oscar, which he won for Best Supporting Actor in the motion picture *The Untouchables*.

Chariots of Fire was the first film in half a century to win the Best Picture Oscar without winning one for its director or any of its actors.

Each Best Supporting Actress Oscar winner from 1978 to 1981 had the initials M.S. (Maggie Smith, Meryl Streep, Mary Steenburgen, Maureen Stapleton).

Alcohol & Cocktails

With an olive, it's a Martini; with an onion, the same drink is known as a Gibson.

An unnamed patron at the Ambassador Hotel in Chicago was the first to put a celery stick in a Bloody Mary; he grabbed the vegetable off a tray and used it as a stirrer, since his drink had arrived without one.

In the early nineteenth century, the Mint Julep rivaled coffee as the morning beverage of choice in the American South.

The late Desi Arnaz of *I Love Lucy* fame is the grandson of one of the gentlemen who founded rum-makers Bacardi & Company.

Rum is naturally colorless; caramel is added to the mixture to make it brown.

Mixologists have learned that "signature" drinks have eye appeal, and that customers will pay more for colorful cocktails.

"Whiskey" (spelled with the letter "e") is what's made in America; "whisky" is the name for the beverage when distilled overseas.

Ordering a drink "neat" is not exactly the same as ordering it "straight up." The former means the booze is poured from the bottle at room temperature; in the latter, the spirit is served chilled, but without ice.

Anagrams

When Homer Hickam's book *Rocket Boys* was made into a motion picture, the title was changed to *October Sky.* Coincidence or not, the two titles are anagrams.

While the religion and the soft drink aren't related, we find it interesting that the letters in *Episcopal* can be rearranged into *Pepsi Cola.*

The letters in the name *Clint Eastwood* can be re-arranged to form something the actor has given us in several of his films: *old west action.*

The mathematical problems *twelve plus one* and *eleven plus two* not only contain the same letters, but have the same solution (13).

Genuine class was what many fans felt that late actor *Alec Guinness* displayed in his stage and screen roles.

Not surprisingly, Tasmanian Devils come from Tasmania. More surprisingly, *Tasmania* has a hellish anagram: *I am Satan*.

During the Doors hit "L.A. Woman," lead singer *Jim Morrison* repeats the phrase *Mr. Mojo risin'*, which is an anagram of the late vocalist's name.

Animal Reproduction

Female gorillas of a certain age go through a period of menopause, similar to human women.

Male seahorses, not the females, are the ones who become pregnant and carry the young.

While human females release only one egg at a time, a codfish may release as many as five million at once.

Armadillos always have quadruplets, and each of the babies is a clone of the others.

By definition, two creatures are members of the same species if their offspring have the ability to reproduce.

At birth, baby blue whales are about 25 feet in length and may weigh in excess of 4,000 lbs.

Most amphibians, fish, and reptiles lay eggs, and a few mammals do. But birds are the only group of vertebrates in which every species is an egg-layer.

Animals

While squirrels have rarely been known to attack people (mostly in an attempt to get food), they are immune to rabies and cannot transmit it to human beings.

A camel may lose up to one third of its body weight after feeding off the fat stored in its hump.

Part of the reason that rat poison is so useful in getting rid of rats is that rats don't have the ability to vomit, and thus can't expel the poison from their bodies.

Squirrels excrete a scent from glands in between the pads in their feet, allowing them to "mark" trees as their own.

If you can smell but can't see cat urine in your home, try turning the lights off and using a black light to closely examine carpeting and furniture. Cat urine will glow under such a light.

If boxing a kangaroo, it's best if you stay behind him. Because of its long tail and the shape of its legs, a kangaroo has a difficult time moving backwards.

In addition to the Tennessee Walking Horse, there's also a breed known as the Missouri Fox-Trotting Horse.

Apples

The first food consumed in outer space (by John Glenn in 1962) was puréed applesauce.

The phrase *laptop machines* is an anagram of *Apple Macintosh*.

While only a few apple types are common in fruit markets, there are about 7,500 varieties of the fruit worldwide.

The indented part of the apple on the bottom, opposite the top stem, is called the calyx.

The fruit appearing on The Beatles' own Apple Records label was a Granny Smith.

While they're certainly healthy for you, apples contain less protein than almost every other fruit. An equivalent amount of cherries, for instance, contains six times as much protein.

An average apple contains five seeds.

Architecture

The dome over Thomas Jefferson's home, Monticello, concealed a game room with a billiards table (the sport was illegal at the time).

Chicago is home to more skyscrapers over 1,000 feet tall than any other U.S. city.

Famous TV architects include Elise Keaton (*Family Ties*), Wilbur Post (*Mr. Ed*), and Mike Brady (*The Brady Bunch*).

Bill Clinton must have felt at home seeing the U.S. Capitol building in Washington; the State Capitol building in his home state of Arkansas is a scaled-down replica of the same structure.

Gun company heiress Sarah Winchester had her 160-room mansion in San Jose built to keep evil spirits away, using odd tricks such as stairways leading to nowhere and blind chimneys.

The Gateway Arch in St. Louis appears taller than it is wide, but only because of an optical illusion. Both measurements are 630 feet.

In order to circumvent building codes, Space Mountain at Disneyland was constructed around a small basketball court.

Around the World

The easternmost point of North America is further east than the westernmost point of the African continent.

Antarctica receives less precipitation than any other continent. The snow there has built up over centuries (as, obviously, it's too cold for it to melt).

Combined, the nations of China and India have more than eight times as many residents as the third most populous country, the United States.

Brazil has twice as much (and Russia three times as much) forest land than the United States.

Nigeria is Africa's most populous nation by a rather wide margin. With nearly 160 million residents, it has twice as many people as second on the list, Ethiopia.

In 1963, sailors off the coast of Iceland watched in wonder as lava from an erupting underwater volcano broke the surface of the ocean and formed a new island (which now covers an area of about one square mile).

There's more to North America than just the United States, Canada, and Mexico; the continent is home to 23 sovereign nations.

Arnold "the Terminator"

Arnold Schwarzenegger served seven days in jail in 1965 for going AWOL from the Austrian army to enter (and win) a bodybuilding contest.

Schwarzenegger's *Terminator* film series has spread over three decades: the first film appeared in 1984, the second hit theaters 1991, and the third was released in 2003.

In his first film, 1970's *Hercules in New York*, Schwarzenegger was billed as Arnold Strong.

Despite his box-office success, Arnold won a special 2005 Razzie Award as "The Worst Loser" over the past 25 years (he'd been nominated for eight Razzies, but had never won).

At 6'2", Arnold was too short to play *The Incredible Hulk* on television, so the role went to 6'5" Lou Ferrigno.

In 1973, Schwarzenegger appeared as a contestant on *The New Dating Game*.

Arnold Schwarzenegger was the first civilian to own his own Humvee vehicle.

Assassination Attempts

The purpose behind Dr. Martin Luther King Jr.'s trip to Memphis in April 1968 was to support the city's striking garbage workers. He was assassinated the night before he was scheduled to lead a protest march.

In 1975, Gerald Ford was the focus of an assassination attempt when Lynette "Squeaky" Fromme, a former member of the Manson Family, pulled a gun on him.

The assassination of Archduke Ferdinand, the event that spiraled into World War I, was performed by a 19-year-old named Gavrilo Princip.

After one of Adolf Hitler's officers planted a briefcase bomb in 1944 that failed to kill him, the German leader filmed the grisly executions of those responsible and showed the footage to his political and military assistants to dissuade further attempts.

One of the persons indicted in 1995 for attempting to hire someone to assassinate Rev. Louis Farrakhan was Qubilah Shabazz, daughter of civil rights leader Malcolm X.

Just as conspiracy theorists question the facts behind JFK's assassination, some believe that Sirhan Sirhan did not act alone in the murder of Kennedy's brother, Robert. They claim that his multiple head wounds weren't consistent with the actions of a lone gunman.

At Ford's Theatre, John Wilkes Booth reportedly waited in the shadows until he heard a stage actor shout the line he knew would make the audience roar with laughter—"You sockdologizing old man-trap!"—before murdering President Abraham Lincoln.

Automakers' Secret Lives

Ransom E. Olds, the founder of Oldsmobile, also invented the power lawnmower.

After selling his automobile manufacturing company in 1915, Louis Chevrolet tried his hand at other forms of transportation, designing and building both boats and airplanes.

Henry Ford found a use for the excess wood and sawdust generated in his factories; he invented charcoal briquettes, which were sold alongside barbecue grills in Ford dealerships.

Just like the Wright Brothers, the Dodge Brothers started out in their transportation careers by making bicycles.

Before he founded Buick Motors, David Buick patented a process for bonding porcelain to iron, giving birth to the modern-day white bathtub.

Edsel Ford was instrumental in convincing his father, Henry, to purchase the assets of the bankrupt Lincoln Motor Company in 1922.

Automobiles by the Numbers (and Letters)

The average two-car family drives 25,000 total miles per year, a distance equal to a trip completely around the world.

Oil doesn't just go in your car, but under your car; it takes about seven gallons of crude oil to produce an automotive tire.

In the mid-1980s, Dodge produced a limited-edition, high-powered version of the Omni called the GLH. The less-than-subtle initials stood for "Goes Like Hell."

The DeLorean Motor Company blew through $175 million of investor money in a little over a year, but only produced about 8,500 cars.

An automobile's gas mileage can be reduced by as much as five percent if the tires are underinflated.

It takes less energy for a passenger to travel one mile by jumbo jet than it does for that same passenger to drive one mile via automobile.

When referencing 10W/30 motor oil, the "W" doesn't stand for "weight," but rather for "winter."

Aviation

An average of 60,000 persons are airborne over the United States at any given moment.

Musicians Otis Redding and Stevie Ray Vaughan were killed in separate Wisconsin aircraft mishaps.

The first flight attendants were required to be licensed nurses; their goal then was not to serve drinks and make announcements, but to help frightened and ill passengers.

The airspace is restricted in the skies above both Disneyland in California and Walt Disney World in Florida.

A U.S. military pilot is as likely to be a member of the Navy as of the Air Force. Each branch has about 6,500 aircraft in use.

In contrast to his stories about time travel and far-off universes, science-fiction author Isaac Asimov wasn't much of an adventurer—he was afraid of flying.

Actress Swoosie Kurtz garnered her unusual first name from the type of plane her father piloted during World War II.

Commercial flights observe a "sterile cockpit" at any altitude less than 10,000 feet. This has nothing to do with germs; it simply bans nonessential personnel and conversation on the flight deck.

Balloons

In 1783, the first three passengers ascended above the Earth in a gondola below a hot-air balloon. The group was comprised of a rooster, a duck, and a sheep.

Larry Walters filled 45 weather balloons with helium and tethered them to a lawn chair in July 1982. He floated 15,000 feet in the air above Los Angeles (and was spotted by two airliners) before returning to Earth in Long Beach.

Richard Branson has set records piloting hot-air balloons, but he wasn't the first mogul to be fascinated by them. Publishing magnate Malcolm Forbes collected unusually shaped hot-air balloons.

Felix the Cat became the first large "character" balloon to appear in the Macy's Thanksgiving Day Parade, back in 1927.

Swiss physicist Auguste Piccard's career experienced both highs and lows. In 1932, he soared 55,000 feet into the air in a balloon. Twenty years later, he descended more than 10,000 feet into the ocean in a bathyscaphe of his own design.

In the world of comic strips, the shapes above characters' heads containing their thoughts and/or words are called "balloons."

The Montgolfier brothers' first public demonstration of a hot-air balloon in 1783 in Annonay, France, was attended by at least one American citizen of note: Benjamin Franklin.

Banking

In 1971, it became a law that every federally insured bank and savings & loan install cameras so that every person approaching a teller was caught on film.

For a joke, Patrick Combs visited an ATM and deposited a $95,000 sample check he received as junk mail in 1995. The bank credited his account and didn't discover the error for more than one month. (He later returned the money.)

7-11 has the largest ATM network of any retailer in the United States.

In 2003, more than 18 million checks went unpaid ("bounced"), according to the Federal Reserve. This represents about 1 in every 200 checks written.

When a person withdraws more than $10,000 from any financial institution in the United States, the IRS is automatically notified.

One of the most popular banks of the 1960s was the Commerce Bank of Beverly Hills. It was there that Milburn Drysdale was put in charge of Jed Clampett's $25 million oil fortune on TV's *The Beverly Hillbillies*.

While the number of ATM transactions made in the United States is the same as it was 10 years ago, the number of automated teller machines has more than tripled to nearly 400,000.

Barefootin'

In 1960, Abebe Bikila became the first black African to win an Olympic gold medal. He was not only victorious in one of the most grueling competitions—the marathon—but he won the race running bare-foot.

Despite being American-born and physically gifted, martial arts legend Bruce Lee was exempt from military service for only one reason: he had flat feet.

Wilbur Young coined the term "athlete's foot" in the 1930s to help sell his new linament, known as Absorbine Jr.

While his shabby clothing didn't garner any notice, Johnny Appleseed (John Chapman) was easy to spot in a crowd due to his bare feet and his favorite headgear—a tin pot.

In the prime-time cartoon *The Flintstones*, our Stone Age ancestors' hands had four digits each (three fingers and a thumb), while each foot only had three toes.

To protect his own feet, Bruce Willis wore a prosthetic pair of foot-shaped boots over his real bare feet while filming *Die Hard*. These can clearly be seen in at least one point in the film.

William Scholl was inspired to go to medical school and earn a podiatry degree only after he noticed that customers at the Chicago shoe store where he worked regularly complained about aches and pains in their feet.

Basketball

The world record for dunking was set by Michael "Wild Thing" Wilson of the Harlem Globetrotters back in 2000, when he performed the feat at a height of 12 feet.

Despite a name that logically would have originated in the "Motor City," Detroit's NBA franchise started out life in Indiana as the Fort Wayne Pistons.

Early rules of the sport of basketball required that each successful field goal be followed by a jump ball.

In 1973, the Philadelphia 76ers set a record not matched in the NBA since, when they lost 20 consecutive games.

Playing for Morningside High in Inglewood, California, Lisa Leslie set a high school basketball scoring record by pouring in all but one of her team's 102 first-half points.

The NBA's Buffalo Braves became the San Diego Clippers in 1978, a climate shock for players who went from one of the nation's coldest, snowiest areas to one of the warmest, driest ones.

Batteries

The first batteries produced for consumers were used to power telephones.

The Energizer Bunny only made his debut in 1989, yet he placed at #5 on *Advertising Age* magazine's list of the "Top 10 Advertising Icons of the Century."

Now popular in small electronic gadgets, AAA-size batteries were originally developed in the 1950s for use in a new Eastman Kodak camera that had a built-in flash.

The letter system for "naming" batteries was developed by the American National Standards Institute, with sizes range from AAAA to G.

Consumers rarely see F and G batteries; they're used to power things like lanterns and electric fences.

Refrigerating alkaline batteries does not extend their shelf life by an appreciable amount (experts say less than 5 percent). If you do chill your batteries, it's best to allow them to reach room temperature before installing them.

Until "wearable" vacuum tube hearing aids hit the market in the 1930s, the battery packs that ran the devices had to be carried or strapped to the body.

Experts recommend that you allow rechargeable NiCad (nickel-cadmium) batteries to completely run down at least once a month. Otherwise, they'll begin to suffer from what's called "memory effect," reducing their life span.

Bears

Polar bear fur is actually transparent. It only looks white because of the way it reflects light. In fact, the skin underneath the fur is dark in color.

Sometimes a bear doesn't "go" in the woods. While taking a winter-long nap, all of a bear's bodily functions slow down, meaning the creature doesn't have to relieve itself until emerging in the spring.

Yogi Bear wasn't an instant star. He made his debut in 1958 as a secondary character on the *Huckleberry Hound* show.

"Bear" in TV's *B.J. and the Bear* was not an ursine, but a chimpanzee. Owner B.J. McKay named him after legendary Alabama football coach Paul "Bear" Bryant.

Due to the inefficiency of their digestive systems, giant panda bears must spend 10 to 16 hours per day feeding.

Several national parks are now using specially trained Karelian Bear Dogs, a breed specially trained to interact with approaching grizzly bears. They have the ability to distract a bear that might otherwise become aggressive with humans.

The largest lake in North America that's *not* one of the Great Lakes is the Great Bear Lake, located in the Northwest Territories of Canada.

The Beatles

"A Hard Day's Night" and "Eight Days a Week" were both inspired by malapropisms uttered un-intentionally by Ringo Starr.

While John was growing up, his guardian, Aunt Mimi, repeatedly admonished him, "The guitar's all very well as a hobby, John, but you'll never make a living with it." He later had that saying inscribed on a plaque for her.

The infamous "butcher cover" photo that originally appeared on The Beatles' U.S.-only album *Yesterday and Today* was titled "Somnambulant Adventure."

Jimmy Nichol filled in for 10 shows during a Beatles tour in 1964 when Ringo Starr fell ill and had to have his tonsils removed. Nichol's oft-repeated phrase, "It's getting better" (when asked how things were going), became a Beatles song title years later.

Only one member of the Beatles never appeared on *Saturday Night Live:* John Lennon.

Ed Sullivan had never heard The Beatles perform when he booked them to appear on his TV show—he'd only seen the enormous screaming crowd waiting to greet them at Heathrow Airport.

George and John were the first Beatles to (inadvertently) try LSD; the two ingested the drug while they sat with their wives at a dinner party hosted by George's dentist, who reportedly slipped it into their coffee without telling them.

Benjamin Franklin

Considered one of the most scholarly men of his era, Ben Franklin first attended school at the age of 8 and dropped out when he was only 10.

Boston-born Ben Franklin only relocated to Philadelphia because he could not find work as a printer in New York City.

At 81 years of age, Ben Franklin was the oldest person to sign the U.S. Constitution.

Before Franklin's image was put on the half-dollar coin in 1948, U.S. Mint director Nellie Ross had been urged to use him on the penny instead (in honor of his "a penny saved …" maxim).

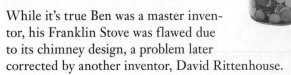

While it's true Ben was a master inventor, his Franklin Stove was flawed due to its chimney design, a problem later corrected by another inventor, David Rittenhouse.

Before being admitted to the Union in 1796, the eastern part of Tennessee was known as the State of Franklin (named after Ben).

Ben Franklin appeared on the very first U.S. postage stamp, an 1847 release with a face value of five cents.

The Bible*

*All facts in this section refer to the King James Version of the Bible, sans the Apocrypha.

The King James Version of the Bible contains over 12,000 different words, nearly one and a half times as many as the Hebrew Bible, and more than double the number of different words in the Greek Bible.

An average of more than 150,000 copies of the Bible are distributed in the United States every single day.

The text of the New Testament was written over a period of about 50 years; the Old Testament, on the other hand, was compiled during a span of approximately 1,000 years.

The word "eternity" appears only once in the Bible: in the fifty-seventh chapter of the Book of Isaiah.

No verse in the Bible contains all 26 letters of the alphabet.

The Bible was not divided into chapters until the mid-thirteenth century, and was not further divided into verses until 1551.

Psalms is the longest book in the Bible (with 150 chapters). It also contains the shortest chapter (Psalm 117) and the longest one (Psalm 119).

Billboard Magazine

The earliest *Billboard* magazine didn't feature music charts, but rather schedules for traveling carnivals.

America, Cream, and Kiss are not only bands who hit the *Billboard* chart; they're also the titles of Prince songs that reached the Hot 100.

The only #1 *Billboard* pop hit recorded by a father-daughter combination was Frank and Nancy Sinatra's "Something Stupid" from 1967.

Billboard magazine now publishes a weekly list of the Top 20 most popular cell phone ringtones.

The Isley Brothers have accomplished the remarkable feat of appearing on the *Billboard* pop music chart at least once in every decade since the 1950s (including the 2000s).

Only one act appeared in the top five on *Billboard*'s pop singles chart for the week of April 4, 1964: The Beatles held all five spots.

Blood

Creatures from outer space have blood of varying compositions and colors. *Star Trek*'s Spock has green blood, while Ming the Merciless, enemy of *Flash Gordon*, has blue blood.

"Blood, sweat, and tears" is a phrase we're all familiar with. Not only did Winston Churchill not originate this line, his phrasing was different. His offer was one of "blood, toil, tears, and sweat."

In the 1960 black-and-white motion picture *Psycho*, chocolate syrup was substituted for blood, as it had what Alfred Hitchcock felt was the perfect consistency.

Officially listed as pneumonia, many historians now believe that the cause of George Washington's death was the "bloodletting" prescribed to cure him of the ailment in 1799.

The drug *warfarin* (marketed as Coumadin), used as a blood thinner for humans, is also a rather effective rat poison.

Dr. Carl Walter's 1948 invention made blood easier and safer to collect and store for future use: he developed the first plastic bags used to hold donated blood.

If both parents of a child have Type O blood, the child will also have Type O blood. At the other end of the spectrum, if one parent has Type A blood and the other Type B blood, the child may have any blood type (A, B, AB, or O).

Board Games

In 1950, three Monopoly tokens were changed; the lantern, purse, and rocking horse were replaced by the dog, horse-and-rider, and wheelbarrow.

The British version of the board game Clue is known as Cluedo, and the victim is Dr. Black instead of Mr. Body.

The dice game Yahtzee was named for the notion that the Canadian couple who invented the game used to play it while cruising around on their yacht.

Alfred Butts, who devised the game known as Scrabble, originally wanted to call the game Lexico.

The Monopoly property known as Marvin Gardens is misspelled; the district in Margate City, NJ, is correctly given as Marven Gardens.

A standard six-sided die has a total of 21 pips (dots) on its sides. Any two opposite sides add up to the number seven.

Boats & Ships

When the Mayflower arrived in America in 1620, permission was given for the group to settle in Virginia. Problems with weather and navigation forced the ship off-course to the north, so the Pilgrims landed in Massachusetts instead.

It's believed that the British call sneakers *plimsolls* because of the resemblance of the rubber edge guards to the Plimsoll lines on the hulls of ships (which indicate the loading limit).

Songwriter Mike Stoller was a passenger aboard the *Andrea Doria* when it sank in 1956. He was rescued and brought to New York, where songwriting partner Jerry Leiber greeted him with the news that Elvis Presley had recorded their song "Hound Dog."

Civil War Admiral David Farragut's famous line, "Damn the torpedoes, full speed ahead!" didn't reference the motorized projectiles of today, but rather explosive mines in the water.

Battleship was played as a paper-and-pencil game for decades before a fabricated plastic version was sold in toy stores.

An explosion aboard the *U.S.S. Maine* in 1898 was blamed on a sneak attack by Spain, causing the Spanish-American War. More than 75 years later, a Navy report revealed that the damage was caused by a fire, not by an offensive strike.

In 1852, the iron paddle steamer *Birkenhead* hit a rock and sank off the coast of South Africa. The captain demanded that the men allow "women and children" to enter the lifeboats first, which became known as the Birkenhead Drill.

Books and Printing

The frequency order of the 12 most-used letters in the English language is: E, T, A, O, I, N, S, H, R, D, L and U, and those were placed on keys on the first two rows of Linotype typesetting machines.

In 1907, Henri Vallienne published *Kastelo de Pro-longo*, the first novel written entirely in Esperanto (which was developed in a failed attempt to unionize European languages).

Mark Twain was the first author to submit a typewritten manuscript (*Life on the Mississippi*). He used a Remington machine.

Hugo Gernsback, the founder of *Amazing Stories* magazine, coined a new word to describe his tales: scientifiction. Over time, the public began pronouncing it "science fiction," and the name stuck.

Ernest Vincent Wright wrote a 50,000-word novel (*Gadsby*) in 1939 without using the letter E.

Paperback books were once made of cheap newsprint, so publishers stained the edges with color to conceal the quality of the paper.

There are only 50 unique words in Dr. Seuss's *Green Eggs and Ham;* he wrote the book on a challenge to prove that an entertaining kids' book could be written with such a limited vocabulary.

Border-Ball

California is home to three NHL hockey teams, while Canada only has six (the Canadiens, Canucks, Flames, Oilers, Senators, and Maple Leafs).

Three times from 1966–1976 the CFL's Grey Cup was fought between teams called the Rough Riders and the Roughriders (Ottawa and Saskatchewan, respectively).

Surprisingly, the first MLB stadium to include metric measurements on its outfield walls wasn't Canadian; it was Riverfront Stadium in Cincinnati, Ohio.

The Canadian Parliament passed an act naming ice hockey Canada's "national sport," but was forced to amend the act to include a mention of lacrosse because of its popularity there.

The NFL is the only one of the four major American pro sports leagues that has yet to place a team in Canada.

Toronto is the only Canadian city to have hosted World Series games. They won the event the only two times they participated, in 1992 and again in 1993.

Bowling

More then two thirds of the 100 million persons who go bowling at least once a year live in the United States.

If you like scoring, five-pin (which is popular in Canada) might be the bowling game of choice for you. Unlike ten-pin bowling where a perfect score is 300, the best five-pin game tops out at 450.

When throwing a "proper" strike, a bowling ball only touches four of the pins: 1, 3, 5, and 9 for a right-hander, and 1, 2, 5, and 8 for a lefty.

Bowling is more popular amongst men than women, but not by as large a margin as you might think. About 53 percent of bowlers are male.

The length of a bowling alley from foul line to the center of the head pin is 60 feet, or six inches shorter than the distance from the pitcher's mound to home plate.

The maximum weight of a bowling ball is 16 lbs., the same as a men's shot put.

Bowling is like golf, in that the person who participates the least usually has the highest score. A bowler throws between 11 and 21 times over the course of a game.

The Brain

Of the billions of neurons in the human body, about half of them are located in the brain.

Brain tissue cannot feel pain. When you have a headache, it's usually due to a blood vessel or a nerve ending in the skull.

Albert Einstein's brain was smaller than average. It was removed prior to his cremation and was kept secretly stored by Dr. Thomas Harvey, who performed the autopsy on the genius's body in 1955.

The hypothalamus is the part of the brain that regulates our "body clock," which (if we're lucky) helps us wake up on time even if our bedside alarm fails to go off.

The size of the area being served means nothing to the brain. The part of the brain that controls facial muscles, for instance, is larger than the part that controls our arms and legs.

The first name of children's literary sleuth "Brains" Benton is Barclay. Six books in the *Brains Benton Mystery* series were published.

There are seven different types of amnesia, ranging from a complete inability to remember anything to the blocking of one particular moment or event.

Brand Name Origins

Originally a sunburn cream, Noxzema earned its name when a customer wrote in to say the stuff had "knocked out [his] eczema."

Paul Orfalea named his copy store after a nickname he'd been given in college (due to his curly hair): Kinko's.

Benjamin Hirsch knew his car polish resulted in a "hard shell finish," but it wasn't until he saw his reflection in the water of Wisconsin's Turtle Creek that its shine inspired him to call it Turtle Wax.

When first opened in 1962 in Santa Barbara, California, it was easy to tell the room rate for Motel 6, since the price in dollars gave the chain its name.

Dixie cups have nothing to do with the American South. When the New York company opened its factory in a building formerly owned by the Dixie Doll Company, the owners chose to keep the name that was already painted above the door.

William Ramsay developed Kiwi shoe polish, which he named in honor of the national bird of New Zealand, where his wife was born.

The name of L'eggs panty hose was a triple play-on-words. "Egg" for the egg-shaped container, "leg" for the part of the body involved, and the apostrophe made the name appear French (and thus perhaps more elegant) in origin.

British Royalty

If Elizabeth II is still queen in September 2015, she'll overtake Victoria to become the longest-reigning monarch in British history.

According to medical records, Queen Victoria suffered from severe menstrual cramps, for which her personal physician prescribed a rather unique treatment: marijuana.

Scotland's King James IV was a wannabe-dentist, and actually paid patients to allow him to learn the trade by letting him work on their teeth.

Members of the British royal family always carry formal black clothing when traveling, so they can be appropriately dressed when returning home in the event of a death in the family.

Royal insiders claim that Queen Elizabeth's size-able handbag contains only enough money to add to the collection plate at church once a week.

Having been born and raised in Hanover (Germany), George I did not speak English when he became Britain's king in 1714.

Eighteenth-century British monarch Queen Anne gave birth to 17 children, all of whom preceded her in death.

The last time Queen Elizabeth II was obliged to perform a curtsey was at the foot of the coffin of her father, George VI.

Buses

The design on the Partridge Family's colorful bus wasn't just a collection of random geometric shapes. It was based on the art of a Dutch painter named Piet Mondrian.

The word "bus" is short for *omnibus*, meaning "for all." The concept of bus routes and lines dates back to horse-drawn coaches.

In the Spice Girls' 1997 motion picture *Spice World*, the quintet's bus driver (Dennis) was portrayed by platinum-selling vocalist Meat Loaf.

Before it was auctioned to the Henry Ford Museum in 2001 for an incredible $427,919, the bus in which Rosa Parks made her celebrated civil rights stand in 1955 was in an Alabama field and was used to store tools and wood.

Hibbing, Minnesota, was the original home of the Greyhound bus line. While Hibbing is now home to a museum housing 11 retired buses, there's currently no Greyhound stop in town.

General Motors held such a monopoly on the nation's bus production that the U.S. Justice Department filed suit in 1956 to force the company to release their patents to competitors, which they finally did nine years later.

School buses are commonly painted a shade called National School Bus Chrome Yellow, and may be white on top to help reflect sunlight and thus keep the vehicle cooler inside.

Carrots

Cartoon voice legend Mel Blanc chewed on carrots to provide an "authentic" sound for Bugs Bunny's mealtime. While he was *not* allergic to the vegetable, he never cared for them, and spit out the chewed remnants instead of swallowing.

While orange carrots are certainly the most common, the vegetable is available in a plethora of colors, including white, yellow, red, green, and purple.

The longest carrot whose length was verified measured nearly 17 feet from stem to tip.

Sure, Scott Thompson (the comedian known as "Carrot Top") uses a lot of gadgets on-stage. His love for them must be hereditary, as his father was an engineer for NASA.

The flowering herb plant known as Queen Anne's Lace is really a wild carrot.

It's true; eating too many carrots will turn the skin an orange shade. While the carotene that causes this is harmless, the associated amounts of vitamin A can be harmful to humans.

The long, thin carrot preferred by consumers in the United States and Canada is the Impersonator Carrot. It isn't as common elsewhere in the world, where shoppers prefer shorter, rounder carrot varieties.

Celebrity Afflictions

Both Hank Williams and John Mellencamp were born with a birth defect known as *spina bifida*.

Researchers identified a "Parkinson's Cluster" of workers involved in the Canadian sitcom *Leo and Me*. Four of them (including Michael J. Fox) went on to develop the disease.

Demi Moore was born with crossed eyes, an affliction corrected in her youth thanks to two surgical procedures.

Cher struggled with dyslexia for many years, and used to have friends read scripts to her so that she could memorize them.

Dolly Parton has it on top, while Danny Devito doesn't … hair, we mean. While they're both five feet tall, Parton's tall wigs make her appear notably taller than the balding Devito.

Tom Cruise has what's called a *fused midline incisor*, meaning that instead of the normal four front teeth in his upper jaw, he only has three.

Worried that news of surgery would panic the nation, President Grover Cleveland had a tumor removed from the roof of his mouth while "resting" on board a yacht in Long Island Sound.

Celebrity Tattoos

Actress Geena Davis has a Denny's Restaurant logo on her ankle—an attempt to cover a tattoo of the first name of her ex-husband, Renny Harlin.

Johnny Depp sports a tattoo on his bicep that reads "Wino Forever;" it originally read "Winona Forever," but Depp had it altered after his engagement to Winona Ryder was called off.

Thomas Edison not only patented the first electric tattoo machine, he also had a tattoo of five dots (like those on the face of dice) on his forearm.

John F. Kennedy, Jr. had a small tattoo of a shamrock inked on his backside, reportedly the result of a wild night spent out "on the town" in Manhattan.

Pamela Anderson had the first name of then-husband (and Mötley Crüe drummer) Tommy Lee tattooed on her ring finger. After their break-up, she had it changed to read "Mommy."

Robert Clary was the only cast member of TV's *Hogan's Heroes* who had actually spent time in a concentration camp. He still has the "A-5714" tattoo he received at Buchenwald on his forearm.

Roseanne eventually had the "Property of Tom Arnold" tattoo covered with another design after their break-up, but not before ex-hubby Tom remarked that the claim made him the fourth-largest property owner in California.

Cereal

Small boxes of Quaker Oats were the first "trial-size" samples offered to the public. In 1890, one was delivered to every mailbox in Portland, Oregon.

The rooster that has long appeared on boxes of Kellogg's Corn Flakes is named Cornelius.

Over the years, we've seen quite a bit of Tony the Tiger's family. His wife is Mrs. Tony, his son is Tony Junior, and his daughter is named Antoinette.

While it more closely resembles a square pillow, the shape of Cap'n Crunch cereal is intended to represent a treasure chest.

Count Chocula, Frankenberry, and Booberry are three of what was originally five "monster" cereals sold by General Mills. The others were Fruit Brute and Yummy Mummy.

In case you have difficulty telling them apart, Snap wears a baker's hat, Crackle dons a stocking hat, and Pop's head is topped with a military hat.

The first male athlete to appear on a Wheaties box was Lou Gehrig in 1934. The first female athlete to earn the honor was Mary Lou Retton, exactly 50 years later.

Child Actors

Children working in the entertainment business are exempt from most child labor laws. In some states, a baby as young as 15 days old can be issued a work permit.

By law, makeup artists have to use food products, and not cosmetics, on infant actors. Even then, care has to be taken to prevent allergic reactions.

Working with babies on a film or TV set is expensive; by law, a nurse has to be present at all times, and special lights have to be used (to protect the infant's eyes).

Most studios use twins (or even triplets) when filming babies since that extends the amount of time they can appear on camera. In addition, if a baby is ill or fussy, a sibling can fill in without having to cancel a planned shoot.

The so-called Coogan Law, which requires that a percentage of a child actor's earnings be put in trust, came about when child star Jackie Coogan turned 18 and found that his parents had squandered his $4 million fortune.

Interestingly enough, line by line, there are more laws and regulations regarding the treatment of animals on a film set than there are for children.

Children's Authors

Carolyn Keene and Franklin Dixon, the authors behind the *Nancy Drew* and *Hardy Boys* book series, never existed. The stories were all penned by other writers under contract.

As a child, Beverly Cleary was put into the lowest reading circle in grade school. She later admitted that this disappointment is what inspired her to become a bestselling kids' author.

Shel Silverstein was more than a kids' author; he drew cartoons for *Playboy* and wrote the lyrics to the Johnny Cash hit song "A Boy Named Sue."

Norman Bridwell originally wanted to give the "Big Red Dog" he created the name Tiny; his wife suggested *Clifford* after the name of her imaginary childhood friend.

H.A. Rey fled Paris via bicycle in 1940 (just prior to the Nazi occupation) with only some food, a few items of clothing, and a manuscript that was later published as *Curious George*.

Harry Potter author J.K. Rowling is a huge fan of the rock band The Smiths. The usually reclusive author appeared in a documentary film concerning the group's lead singer, Morrissey.

Christmas Carols

Ray Evans and Jay Livingston, who
composed the *Mr. Ed* theme song,
are also the authors of the Christmas
classic "Silver Bells."

Mel Torme wrote "The Christmas
Song" (often referred to as "Chestnuts
Roasting over an Open Fire") during a
blistering heat wave in July 1946.

"We Three Kings of Orient Are,"
which tells the Biblical story of Matthew 2:1-11,
was written in 1857 by John Henry Hopkins as a
Christmas present for his nieces and nephews.

"Jingle Bells" was written as a tribute to the winter
sport of sleigh racing. Composer James Pierpont
had originally titled his song "The One-Horse
Open Sleigh."

The melody for "Hark! The Herald Angels Sing"
was composed by Felix Mendelssohn in 1840 as
part of a celebration commemorating the invention
of the printing press.

James R. Murray used a poem he found in an 1885
Lutheran school book to write the classic "Away in
a Manger."

Lock your doors if you hear singers belting out
"Here We Come A-Wassailing." Wassail is a potent
warm brew of ale or wine flavored with cinnamon,
apples, and nutmeg.

Cigarettes & Tobacco

Originally intended for women, Marlboro introduced "red-tipped" cigarettes in 1936 to hide lipstick marks.

Virginia Slims was the last brand of cigarettes promoted on TV before such ads were banned in 1971.

Bright, Burley, and Oriental are the three varieties of tobacco commonly blended to produce most U.S. cigarettes.

Joe, the dromedary depicted on packages of Camel cigarettes since the brand began in 1913, was a featured attraction in the Barnum & Bailey Circus.

During the Civil War, soldiers would sometimes sneak over enemy lines for secret one-on-one trading opportunities. Not surprisingly, one of the hottest commodities was Rebel tobacco.

As the cartoon was originally intended for adults, Winston cigarettes served as sponsor for the first two seasons of *The Flintstones*.

The Civil War

Short of supplies, the South was forced to find substitutes for necessities like coffee. Ground acorns were a common substitute.

Abraham Lincoln wasn't the featured speaker at the dedication of the Gettysburg National Cemetery.

His two-minute speech followed a two-hour oration by Edward Everett.

U.S. Senator John Crittendon of Kentucky was the father of two major generals who served during the Civil War (one for the Union, one for the Confederacy).

During the Civil War, hot air balloons were used for surveillance. This marked the first time that aircraft were used by the U.S. military.

When the Civil War broke out in 1861, the Union invalidated all existing postage stamps to ensure that the South could not cash in those that had been confiscated by the new Confederate government. New stamps were printed (and distributed only in the North).

Estimates claim that as many as two thirds of the military men who died during the Civil War fell victim to disease rather than battle injuries.

To help fund the cost of the war, the U.S. Congress enacted the first income tax in 1862. The standard rate was 3 percent.

Clubs & Organizations

The Rotary Club earned its name by rotating the location of the organization's meetings throughout the membership, from office to office.

While experts believe it was Venus, former president Jimmy Carter claims to have seen a UFO in the sky just prior to attending a Lions Club meeting in 1969.

Among musical "organizations" that have hit the Pop Top-40 are: Breakfast Club, Club Nouveau, Culture Club, The Escape Club, Timex Social Club, and Tom Tom Club.

The four H's in the 4-H Club originally stood for Head, Heart, Hands, and Hustle. The final H was changed to "Health" at a national meeting in Washington, D.C., in 1911.

Both *The Mickey Mouse Club* and *Captain Kangaroo* premiered on October 3, 1955. The former was cancelled after four years, while Bob Keeshan and company stayed on the air for just short of three decades (until 1984).

Before it adopted the Native American name in 1915, the Kiwanis Club was known as BOB— the Benevolent Order Brothers.

Franklin D. Roosevelt, whose profile appears on the dime coin, was one of the founders of the polio-fighting organization that came to be known (not coincidentally) as the March of Dimes.

Coffee

A&P's signature coffee brand, Eight O'clock, was named after a survey in which Americans revealed that was the time of morning most coffee was consumed.

Canadians drink more coffee on a per-capita basis than any other nation on Earth.

You can't get that coffee flavor "fresh off the plant." It's the roasting of the beans that gives coffee the flavor with which we're familiar.

William Black owned a NYC nut store known as Chock Full o' Nuts. When sales plummeted during the Great Depression, he switched to selling coffee, but kept his company's name.

According to legend, a goatherd named Kaidi "discovered" coffee in the ninth century after noticing that his goats became excited after eating berries from wild coffee bushes.

Caffeine is on the International Olympic Committee's list of banned substances. A half-dozen cups of coffee might be enough to bar an athlete from competition.

Sanka, the first decaffeinated coffee brand, offered orange pots to promote their product to restaurants when it was first introduced. To this day, the color is synonymous with "decaf" in most eateries.

Cold

The coldest measured temperature in the world occurred in July 1983, when the mercury dipped to 89.2° below zero at the Vostok Base in Antarctica.

James Brown's 1967 song "Cold Sweat" is popularly considered to be the birth of funk music.

Over-the-counter remedies are a $700 million per year business, which is one of several reasons scientists haven't been in a hurry to find a cure for the common cold.

When we're cold, the tiny muscles surrounding our hair follicles contract, making our bodily hairs stand up, which would keep us warm if we were covered with fur. They're called "goose bumps."

Wrestler Steve Austin got the idea for his nickname one day when his wife admonished him to drink his tea before it got "stone cold."

Cold duck, the beverage combo of burgundy wine and champagne, has nothing to do with fowl. Its odd appellation is a translation of its original German name, Kalte Ente.

When it comes to cold cuts, Americans are fonder of ham than any other meat.

Colleges & Universities

Unable to afford bricks, Booker T. Washington had students fire their own clay bricks to build the Tuskegee Institute.

Don't call them the Cardinals; a team from Stanford University is properly called the Cardinal (singular) for their school color.

Traced back to the University of Michigan in 1952, the first "panty raids" were known as "lace riots."

It wasn't until 1978 that all of the "Seven Sisters" schools were headed by female presidents.

Harvard University was founded in 1636, just 16 years after the Mayflower reached the American shore.

Each member of the rock band Queen was a college graduate (their diplomas were in art, astronomy, biology, and electronics).

Sports historians believe the football huddle was introduced in 1894 at Gallaudet University, a school for the hearing impaired.

Comic Strips & Comic Books

Feline comic strip character Garfield once claimed that *Old Yeller* was his favorite motion picture, thanks in no small part to its "happy ending."

In 1977, the four members of KISS mixed their blood in with the ink used to print a Marvel comic book featuring the hard rock band.

For years, a sibling combo has appeared in different strips in newspapers around the country: the title soldier from *Beetle Bailey* is the brother of Lois Flagston of *Hi & Lois*.

Per the original story, Lex Luthor was a high school friend of Superman; the Man of Steel inadvertently caused Lex to lose his hair, forever turning him against the hero.

Charles Schulz's *Peanuts* was originally known as *Li'l Folks*. Due to potential trademark issues, the title was changed when the comic strip was first syndicated, against the artist's wishes.

In 1988, Batman's sidekick, Robin, was killed off after readers voted for his demise in a telephone poll.

The nonsense characters that stand in for swear words in cartoons and comics are known as *grawlix*.

Cookies

Fortune cookies were neither invented in China nor by the Chinese. They were introduced in 1914 by Makoto Hagiwara at the Japanese Tea Garden in San Francisco.

The strings on boxes of Barnum's Animal Crackers are meant to be used to hang them from Christmas trees.

Oreo wasn't the first crème-filled chocolate cookie treat; the very similar Hydrox brand beat them to the punch by two years.

Sadly, former cookie maker Wally "Famous" Amos fell victim to financial difficulties and was actually forced to sign away his rights to the use of his own likeness on products.

The oft-repeated story of the shopper who was charged hundreds of dollars for a cookie recipe only to feel obligated share it for free over the Internet in retribution, is just that: a (false) story.

Per a policy implemented by the organization's national board, Girl Scout Cookies may not be sold online, either on scout-related web pages or on Internet auction sites.

Sylvester Graham developed the crackers that bear his name in the early nineteenth century. Puritan groups were the first to purchase them, believing Graham's claim that eating them helped to reduce sexual urges.

Corny Trivia

The average ear of corn has 800 kernels arranged geometrically into 16 rows.

According to legend, Dolly Parton's parents were so poor that they paid the doctor who delivered her in cornmeal instead of cash.

Botanists have, over several decades, developed thousands of corn hybrids best suited for certain uses, certain soils, and certain weather conditions.

Cicely Tyson, not Bo Derek, was the first Hollywood star to sport cornrows in her hair.

An ear of corn contains about 80 percent water.

While the gasoline substitute known as "ethanol" is made from corn in the United States, it's made from sugar cane in Brazil.

Promoting corn chips, the Frito Bandito was taken off the air after Hispanics complained about the stereotypical image.

While "corn" in America means the specific vegetable, "corn" is commonly used in Britain to generically refer to any grain crop, such as oats or wheat.

The Cosby Show

In later seasons of *The Cosby Show*, Bill regularly wore on his clothing a button with the letters "SD" on it, in tribute to his friend Sammy Davis Jr.

Then-21-year-old Whitney Houston was one of the finalists for the role of the eldest Huxtable daughter, Sondra.

Samuel L. Jackson was Bill Cosby's stand-in during filming of *The Cosby Show* from 1985 to 1989.

In the pilot episode of *The Cosby Show*, the Huxtables had only four children. This was changed to five with the addition of Sabrina LeBeauf (Sondra) to the cast.

The role of Rudy on *The Cosby Show* was originally written for a boy.

Throughout the series' run, the first name of Cliff Huxtable was alternately given as Clifford, Heathcliff, and Heathclifford.

Country Music

The *Grand Ole Opry* has been going strong since 1925, making it the longest-running live radio show in American history.

Eddy Arnold hit the *Billboard* country charts regularly during his long career. He chalked up 145 single hits, including 28 number ones and an incredible 92 top-ten songs.

Country singer John Conlee, who hit #1 with "Backside of Thirty" and "In My Eyes," once held a job that people were dying to be a part of: he was a licensed embalmer.

At the age of 15, Hank Williams Jr. provided the vocal parts for his father's songs as they appeared in the 1964 film about his life, *Your Cheatin' Heart*.

After a long career rooted firmly in country music, the late Tammy Wynette's last Top-40 hit was the 1992 dance song "Justified and Ancient," sung with a British electronica band known as The KLF.

Backlash hit the country music industry when Olivia Newton-John won a series of awards in the mid-1970s (including a Grammy), since she was born in Britain and not America.

Louis Marshall Jones was a morning radio personality who developed his best-known character at the age of 22. From then on, he was known as "Grandpa" Jones.

Creatures Great & Small

Elephants can suck gallons of water into their trunks, but they have to squirt it into their mouths in order to swallow the liquid.

While some are close, no land animal would probably get a ticket on an open Interstate highway. The fastest is the cheetah, clocked at 64 mph.

Marsupials aren't limited to only kangaroos, koalas, and opossums. In fact, the order is made up of more than 250 different species.

Fish named after other creatures include the boarfish, butterfly fish, catfish, parrotfish, rabbit fish, squirrelfish, and toadfish.

Despite its ferocious name, the Tanzanian parasitic wasp has a wingspan of less than $\frac{1}{100}$ of an inch, making it the world's tiniest winged insect.

Not all plankton is harmless; a species known as *Pfiesteria piscicida* releases a toxin in the water that can kill creatures in its vicinity.

While fewer than 5,000 bacteria species have been identified, bacteriologists believe that there may be millions more that have yet to be classified.

Credit Cards

Like many names familiar to consumers (from Craftsman to Allstate), the Discover Card was a creation of Sears, Roebuck & Company. It was introduced in 1985 and spun off from the company a decade later.

MasterCard's corporate headquarters are located in a city with a very appropriate name: Purchase, New York.

Unsecured credit card debt more than doubled (from under $300 billion to over $650 billion) from 1992 to 2000.

Until 1969, the American Express card was purple, after which it was changed to green to reflect the color of U.S. money. Today's cards are available in a variety of colors, depending on the type.

Early credit cards issued by major department stores were called *charge-a-plates*.

The first multi-use charge card (accepted by different retail establishments) was the Diner's Club card, launched in 1950 by Frank McNamara.

By 1980, they were known as MasterCard and Visa. In 1975, however, the same two cards were known as Master Charge and BankAmericard.

Dance

The *Charleston* was innovative in that it was one of the few dances of the era that could be performed either as a couple or alone.

After the *polka* became a popular dance, the name was used to promote many other products. That's how the fabric patterns with large circles on them became known as polka dots.

The album *A Collection of Great Dance Songs* isn't what you might think. Instead of featuring waltz music or the latest techno beats, the 1983 record was a compilation of tunes by prog-rock stars Pink Floyd.

The stiff *Riverdance* movements hearken back to the eighteenth century when Irish step-dancing was illegal. By keeping the upper body stiff, it would not appear to lawmen peering through the windows that anyone was dancing.

A short list of dances named after real or fictional persons:

The Foxtrot (Harry Fox)
The Bartman (Bart Simpson)
The Freddie (Freddie & the Dreamers)
The Humpty Dance (Humpty Hump, a.k.a. Shock-G)
The Soupy Shuffle (Soupy Sales)
The Urkel (Steve Urkel)
The Lindy Hop (Charles Lindbergh)

Deserts

The Sahara Desert is massive, covering a 3.5 million-square-mile area of land that is nearly the same size as the United States.

Ürümqi, a city of more than one million residents located in an oasis in the middle of desert land in western China, is farther from the nearest large body of water than any other major city.

Nearly one third of the Earth's land area is desert (most of it in the Sahara, Australia, and Antarctica). That amount is increasing every year.

"Desert" doesn't necessarily imply heat. By definition, it's an area of sparse vegetation that receives less than 10 inches of rain a year.

The Atacama Desert in Chile is perhaps the driest place on the face of the Earth. It's not uncommon for a full year to pass there without even a trace of precipitation.

While there are dry regions in Europe, it's considered the only continent on Earth without a true desert.

Nearly 80 percent of the surface area of the Sahara Desert isn't sand, but exposed rock.

Detroit

Designated as State Highway 1, Detroit's Woodward Avenue was the first paved road in the United States.

More crossings occur between Detroit and Windsor, Ontario, than at any other point on the United States-Canada border.

Once the fourth-largest city in the United States with about 1.7 million inhabitants, Detroit has lost more than half its population since 1950 and now ranks outside the top 10.

Prior to founding Motown Records, Berry Gordy held a rather typical Detroit job, on a Ford assembly line.

During Prohibition, the frigid Michigan weather helped Detroit-area bootleggers, who would drive their cars back and forth across the frozen Detroit River to smuggle alcohol in from Canada.

In 1980, after making donations to Detroit, Iraqi president Saddam Hussein was presented with a key to the city.

Folks in downtown Detroit heading across the border to Canada have to go south, not north, to reach Windsor, Ontario.

Disney Facts

Walt Disney's *Snow White and the Seven Dwarfs* was the first-ever feature-length animated motion picture.

Disney entered into serious negotiations with Jim Henson to buy out his production company in 1989. The Muppet creator's untimely passing one year later stalled the deal, which finally went through in 2004.

The familiar Disney logo was designed by an artist and bears no resemblance to Walt Disney's real signature.

As of 2006, Disney's 1991 feature *The Lion King* is still the highest-grossing standard-animation film released in the United States.

Despite rumors to the contrary, Walt Disney's body was not cryogenically frozen following his death. His remains are interred alongside those of many other celebrities at Forest Lawn Cemetery in Glendale, California.

Though the rule was only selectively enforced, Disneyland's dress code forbade long-haired men from entering the theme park until the late 1960s.

In addition to his children's fare, Walt Disney produced films for other purposes as well. His efforts included World War II propaganda movies as well as other oddities like the health-minded 1946 short, *The Story of Menstruation*.

Dogs

It's no accident that Fido became a generic name for a dog; it's based on the Latin for "I am faithful."

The first Akita dog brought to America was a puppy that a Japanese policeman gave as a gift to Helen Keller in 1937.

The greyhound is the only dog mentioned by breed in the King James Version of the Bible.

A dog ages the equivalent of 10 human years for the first 2 years of its life, then about 4 human years each year thereafter.

Singer Cat Stevens belied his name with his first single, which was titled "I Love My Dog."

Most veterinarians recommend against feeding your dog a vegetarian diet. Dogs are natural carnivores and may develop intestinal gas problems when subjected to a meatless diet.

Rock band Three Dog Night was named after the manner in which Australian natives kept warm by sleeping with their canine pets.

Drugs in Weird Places

A narcotic liquid was once found in the center portion of heads of lettuce, a natural occurrence that was bred out of the vegetable over several decades.

Both *Murphy Brown* and *Roseanne* aired episodes in which the sitcom's title character uses marijuana.

Coca-Cola wasn't the only soft drink to at one time contain a drug derivative in its mixture; lithium was once part of the formula for 7-Up.

A Colombian drug-smuggling ring broken up by the DEA in 2006 involved packets of heroin that had been surgically implanted into puppies.

Thomas Jefferson's earliest drafts of the Declaration of Independence were written on paper made from hemp (the same plant that can be harvested as marijuana).

Around the turn of the twentieth century, Bayer marketed heroin as a cough suppressant alongside its other new "miracle drug," aspirin.

Eggs

Just as a hen may produce a double-yolk egg on rare occasions, they may also lay an egg containing no yolk at all.

The beverage known as an *egg cream* doesn't contain any egg at all, only chocolate, cream, and seltzer.

Paul McCartney & Wings' *Back to the Egg* album won the former Beatle a Grammy award in what was, for him, a new category: Best Rock Instrumental, for "Rockestra Theme."

Chicken eggs aren't sorted by size, but by weight. "Large" eggs, the standard size referenced in most recipes, average two ounces each.

Nearly a decade before *Saturday Night Live's* Coneheads donned similarly shaped prosthetic heads, Vincent Price appeared as arch villain Egghead on TV's *Batman*.

Nutritionally, there are no notable differences between white-shelled eggs and brown-shelled eggs.

If cooked at too high a temperature, scrambled eggs may actually turn green (although the color change is harmless to humans).

Eight-Legged Creatures

A conjoined cat, born in Norway in 2001, had only one head but two bodies (with eight legs and two tails). While photos of the creature made the rounds on the Internet, the misshapen kitten died shortly after birth.

Spiders aren't the only arachnids with eight legs. Among the 60,000 species in the class are several varieties of mites, scorpions, and ticks.

A huge, purple octopus named Al is lowered from the rafters at Joe Louis Arena during home games as the mascot of the Detroit Red Wings. Rabid fans have been known to throw octopi on the ice after the team scores a goal, particularly during playoff games.

The Eight Legged Groove Machine sounds like a cheesy 1970s film, but it was in fact the 1988 debut album for British band The Wonder Stuff.

Odin, the supreme god of Norse mythology, was said to ride an eight-legged horse named Sleipnir.

For actor Alfred Molina, both his first and his biggest film roles involved eight-legged creatures.

Spiders petrified him in his first credited appearance (1981's *Raiders of the Lost Ark*), and he portrayed villain Doctor Octopus in the 2004 hit *Spider-Man 2*.

In February 2006, three cats mysteriously died at a National Auto Service Center in Tampa Bay. Poison seemed the likely cause until employees spotted the culprit: a seven-inch-long emperor scorpion.

Famous Last Words

Dustin Hoffman read that Pablo Picasso's last words were "Drink to me." He challenged Paul McCartney to write a song using the phrase, which the former Beatle did for the Wings album *Band on the Run*.

According to Karl Marx's housekeeper, who asked him if he wanted to say anything prior to his passing, the socialist replied, "Last words are for fools who haven't said enough."

Having fallen ill at Hollywood's Roosevelt Hotel, boxer Max Baer Sr. called down to the front desk. When asked if he'd like to see a house doctor, he replied, "No, I need a people doctor." Those were the last words he ever said.

Thomas A. Grasso, an Oklahoma inmate just about to be put to death via lethal injection, was of one mind in his final moments. His last words were: "I did not get my Spaghetti-O's. I got spaghetti. I want the press to know this."

On his deathbed, King Charles II of England wasn't concerned with his wife or his nation. He instructed his brother James not to "let poor Nelly starve," referring to His Majesty's mistress, Eleanor Gwyn.

When a dying Joan Crawford's housekeeper began praying at her bedside, the star reportedly snapped at her: "Don't you dare ask God to help me!"

John Adams's reported last words were "Jefferson survives," believing that his fellow statesman was still alive. In fact, Thomas Jefferson had passed away only a few hours earlier, but the news had not yet arrived.

Fast Food

Two notable differences exist between a McDonald's cheeseburger and one from Burger King: the former has onions, while the latter is served on a sesame seed bun.

The "RB" for which Arby's restaurants were named does not stand for "roast beef" as is widely thought, but for the company's founders, the Raffel Brothers.

On February 9, 2006, Pizza Hut purchased an hour-long slot on 115 major-market radio stations to promote its newest concoction, Cheesy Bites Pizza.

Thanks to the proliferation of inexpensive Mexican fast-food restaurants nationwide, Mexican food consumption in the United States has more than tripled since the mid-1970s.

Colonel Harlan Sanders wasn't a military man; the Indiana-born KFC entrepreneur was awarded an honorary "Kentucky Colonel" title by the governor of the Bluegrass State.

The daughter for whom Wendy's founder Dave Thomas named his restaurant chain wasn't really named Wendy; that was her nickname. Her real name is Melinda.

Feet & Shoes

At the age of 12, Shaquille O'Neal was bigger than most adults, at 5'10" and wearing a 10.5-size shoe. Today, he's 7'1" tall and his feet have grown to a size 22.

A bear cub rescued from a New Mexico wildfire in 1950 was nicknamed Hot Foot Teddy. The U.S. Forestry Service "adopted" the bear as a living version of the fire-prevention character they'd introduced six years prior: Smokey the Bear.

The martial art known as *tae kwon do* literally means "way of foot and fist."

In the last episode of TV's *Cheers*, the ponderous question of the meaning of life was bantered about the bar. Mail carrier and trivia buff Cliff Clavin summed it up using only two words: "Comfortable shoes."

H.J. Heinz came up with the idea of using "57 flavors" in his company's advertising after seeing a sign put up by a shoe store, promoting its "21 styles."

The feathered shoe used as the logo for Goodyear is known as the "Wingfoot."

While they're much more common in today's NFL, star punt returner Billy Johnson's pale cleats were so unusual when he began wearing them in high school during the late 1960s that they earned him the nickname "White Shoes."

Fingers and Hands

Fingernails of the longest (middle) fingers grow fastest; those of the shortest (pinky) fingers the slowest.

The last two living Beatles also happen to be the two left-handed members of the group: Paul McCartney and Ringo Starr.

According to the Bible, Goliath wasn't the only giant in David's neck of the woods. In II Samuel, David's nephew killed a giant that had six fingers on each hand and six toes on each foot.

A Somalia native named Hussain Bisad has what are thought to be the largest hands in the world. From wrist to fingertip, they measure just over 10.5 inches.

The first pitcher inducted to the Baseball Hall of Fame with a losing record was a reliever with a name very appropriate to his position: Rollie Fingers.

A horse's height is measured in hands (four inches each) and fingers (one inch each).

"First" Facts

The cover of the first *TV Guide* in 1953 showcased a person who, at the time, had never once appeared on the small screen: Desi Arnaz Jr.

Pilgrims at the first Thanksgiving used spoons, knives, and … their fingers, as forks weren't in common use at the time.

The 1925 film *The Lost World* was not only the first feature-length film to use stop-motion animation, it was also the first in-flight film shown aboard a commercial aircraft.

The world's first 911 call didn't come from the White House or some major city, but from tiny Haleyville, Alabama.

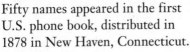

Fifty names appeared in the first U.S. phone book, distributed in 1878 in New Haven, Connecticut.

Time magazine's first "Woman of the Year" was Wallis Simpson, an American divorcée who wed Britain's King Edward VIII, who abdicated the throne for her.

In 1923, the first commercial neon sign promoted Packard automobiles.

First Lady Foibles

Sarah Polk was a devout Presbyterian, and as such, did not dance with her husband, President James Knox Polk, at his Inaugural Ball.

Lucy Hayes was the consummate hostess, but being a staunch temperance advocate, she did not allow any alcohol to be served at White House functions. This earned her the nickname Lemonade Lucy.

Lou Henry Hoover had a fascination with rocks and minerals, and was the first female in the United States to earn a college degree in geology.

Nellie Taft was the first First Lady to be buried alongside her husband in Arlington National Cemetery; the second was Jacqueline Kennedy.

Rosalynn Carter caused tongues to wag when she slipped off her shoes and greeted visiting dignitaries in her stocking feet at the party following her husband's inauguration in 1977.

Although she'll forever be known as Lady Bird (a name she'd acquired as a child), Claudia is the real first name of the wife of the late Lyndon Johnson.

Barbara Bush received sacks of mail complimenting her on her "womanly" figure (in comparison to her reed-slim predecessors). Many times when she was photographed eating a dessert, she'd explain, "I owe it to my public."

Flowers

Don't remove the thorns from roses; doing so makes the flowers susceptible to bacterial infections.

Vanilla, that yummy extract that makes cakes and cookies smell and taste so good, comes from orchids. Farmers pollinate the flowers by hand to ensure a good crop.

The song "Flowers in the Rain" by The Move was the first tune ever played on Radio One, the BBC's first pop music station, when it premiered back in 1967.

If your florist requires that you pay extra for the addition of Baby's Breath to a corsage or arrangements, you're actually being charged for a plant that's considered a weed.

"Frogs" are important to flower arrangements. Not the amphibian type, these "frogs" are the foam or plastic bases hidden inside vases that keep the stems straight.

Many flowers are edible. Chrysanthemums and marigolds have a spicy flavor; nasturtiums resemble radishes in taste, and rose petals are slightly sweet.

Orchids can be found in nearly every color from white to black, with the exception of blue (which has been emulated with a crossbreed of magenta and violet).

Food Name Origins

The Caesar salad is attributed to Caesar Cardini, a restaurateur in Tijuana, Mexico, who created the unusual mix of greens when he was running low on ingredients and used what was left in his refrigerator.

Reuben Kulakofsky of Omaha, Nebraska, is credited with creating the sandwich we now call the Reuben. He first concocted it to feed some late-night poker players at a local hotel.

Bob Cobb, owner of Hollywood's famous Brown Derby restaurant, invented the Cobb salad one night in 1937 when he threw some ingredients from his icebox together to make himself a quick snack.

The Dagwood sandwich is a creation of *Blondie* cartoonist Chic Young. The very first Dagwood consisted of tongue, onion, mustard, sardines, beans, and horseradish.

Oscar Tschirky mixed together chopped apples and celery for the grand opening of New York's Waldorf Hotel in 1893, and created a new salad in the process.

There is some debate over the origin of the club sandwich, but most of the evidence points to the Saratoga Club in Saratoga, New York, where it was first served in the late 1890s.

Green Goddess salad dressing was invented in the early 1920s by the chef at San Francisco's Palace Hotel. He named his creation after the play that was running at the theater across the street at the time.

In the United States, olives are available in seven different sizes. They are: small, medium, large, extra large, jumbo, colossal, and super colossal. In Europe, there are 13 different sizes.

Football

As of 2006, only seven NFL teams didn't have cheerleading or dance squads: the Bears, Browns, Giants, Jets, Lions, Packers, and Steelers.

Los Angeles has been home to four major-league pro football teams, all of which either disbanded or moved away: the Dons, the Chargers, the Rams, and the Raiders.

In 1895, John Brallier became the first "professional" football player in America. He earned a total of $10 plus expenses for the year.

The two-point conversion is the newest scoring option in college football; the rule will have been on the books 50 years in 2008.

Rosey Grier's favorite hobby has long been needle-point. As one of the NFL's first stars to weigh in the 300-lb. range, it's doubtful that anyone dared to make fun of him.

Jim Bakken's 1967 record of seven field goals in an NFL game (for the then-St. Louis Cardinals) has been tied three times, but never broken.

Under early American football rules, a touchdown and a field goal were worth the same number of points (four).

Game Shows

The 1970s game show *Musical Chairs* was the first to feature an African-American host. The show's vocal group (still a few years away from success) was Sister Sledge.

Richard Dawson isn't the *Family Feud* host's real name. He was born Colin Emm.

Years before he became the host of *The Gong Show*, Chuck Barris developed several popular game shows, including *The Dating Game* and *The Newlywed Game*.

Actress Betty White was one of the celebrities who appeared on the third taping of the game show *Password* with Alan Ludden. The two fell in love and were married in 1963.

Before *The Price is Right* broke the record for longest-running daily game show in 1991, the position was held by *Truth or Consequences.* Both shows were hosted by Bob Barker.

Michael Larson carefully studied the patterns in the board used in the game show *Press Your Luck* and took advantage of this knowledge to rack up more than $100,000 in winnings in 1984.

Like Wink Martindale, Dick Clark, and a few other game show hosts, *The Newlywed Game* host Bob Eubanks was also involved in music. He mortgaged his house in 1964 in order to book The Beatles to play a concert at the Hollywood Bowl.

Garbage

On average, more than 1,500 lbs. of trash is generated annually by every man, woman, and child in the United States.

Oscar the Grouch, the icky green *Sesame Street* character who makes his home in a garbage can, was originally orange.

The garbage generated by the United States each year includes up to 20 billion disposable diapers.

From 1970 to 1995, the amount of garbage in the United States increased about 80 percent, while the number of landfills in the nation decreased by the same level.

Estimates reveal that as much as one quarter of the food produced in America annually is lost to spoilage or nonuse.

Per the Ocean Conservancy, nearly 30 percent of the garbage in the world's oceans consists of remnants of cigarettes (mostly the filters).

Giraffes

Contrary to popular belief, giraffes do have vocal cords, though they rarely use them.

It's difficult for a giraffe to lower its head to drink from a river or lake, so the creature gets most of its needed moisture from eating tree leaves.

Melman the giraffe, from the film *Madagascar*, was *Friends* star David Schwimmer's first role voicing an animated character.

Giraffes have been clocked running at speeds up to 35 mph.

Despite the length of its neck, a giraffe has only seven neck vertebrae, the same as humans or any other mammals.

Because of the heart power required to pump blood up its long body, the giraffe has the highest blood pressure of any mammal.

The giraffe was originally known as the camelopard, due to its resemblance to both a camel (in shape) and a leopard (due to the spots on its fur).

Glasses

In 2003, rock legend Elton John had corrective surgery on his eyes to eliminate his need for the 4,000 pairs of eyeglasses he'd collected over the years.

While eyeglasses date back to the thirteenth century, it wasn't until about 450 years later (in 1727) that Edward Scarlett came up with idea of attaching bars to fit over the ears to help hold the glasses on the face.

The 1960 motion picture *Thirteen Ghosts* was shown in what was called Illusion-O, which required the audience to wear special glasses to see the ghouls onscreen.

Eskimos have for centuries made lens-free eyeglasses with very narrow see-through slits in order to protect the wearer's eyes from the constant glare of the sun off ice and snow.

Opticians make and/or sell glasses. Optometrists perform eye tests. Ophthalmologists (also known as oculists) treat diseases of the eye.

The wire-rimmed corrective lens for one eye is called a *monocle*. The style seems to be popular amongst top-hat wearers, including The Penguin, Mr. Peanut, and Charlie McCarthy.

A typical prescription for eyeglasses provides details for O.S. (*oculus sinister*, or "left eye") and O.D. (*oculus dexter*, the right eye).

The Golden Gate

After hard hats were invented in 1919, the first "hard-hat area" was designated at the site of the construction of the Golden Gate Bridge.

The Golden Gate Bridge is not gold in color; the paint used is known as International Orange.

John Charles Frémont named the Bay Area strait the Golden Gate in 1846, before gold was discovered in the region.

A safety net installed under the Golden Gate Bridge helped to cut in half the number of deaths that were expected to occur during its construction. Only 11 men were killed.

Since the mid-1980s, the Golden Gate National Recreation Area has been the second-most-visited unit in the National Park System (behind only the Blue Ridge Parkway).

The Golden Gate Bridge is held up by two 7,650-foot cables. Each cable is wound with 92 strands of steel, and each strand consists of more than 27,500 individual wires.

Gone with the Wind

Barbara O'Neill, who portrayed mother Ellen O'Hara in the motion picture *Gone with the Wind*, was only three years older than Vivien Leigh, who played her daughter, Scarlett.

Georgia segregation laws precluded Hattie McDaniel ("Mammy") from attending the film's world premier at Loew's Grand Theater in Atlanta. Rather than suffer the indignity of not being invited, she sent word that she would be "unavailable" that evening.

Stage hands painted rib "shadows" on a horse in the film in order to give it the gaunt appearance it would have had if malnourished.

Among those who David O. Selznick screen-tested for the role of Mammy was Elizabeth McDuffie, an aspiring actress who had another job at the time: she was a cook for FDR in the White House.

The American Film Institute voted the line "Frankly, my dear, I don't give a damn!" as the number-one movie quote in motion picture history.

Gone with the Wind author Margaret Mitchell spoke out about both of the leads cast in the motion picture:

> When British-born Vivien Leigh beat out New York-born Paulette Goddard for the role of Scarlett O'Hara, Mitchell quipped: "Better an English girl than a Yankee."

> She was less kind after learning that Clark Gable had won the role of Rhett Butler, remarking that she felt he was "all wrong" for the part.

Graves

Hubert Eaton, the founder of Forest Lawn Memorial Parks, came up with the concept of having markers flush with the ground, in order to give the area a more "parklike" feel. (It also simplifies maintenance of the grass.)

For 27 years, until his death in 1999, Joe DiMaggio arranged for fresh roses to be sent to Marilyn Monroe's memorial site in Westwood Memorial Park on a weekly basis.

A stone block had to be placed over Jim Morrison's grave in Paris' Cimetière du Père Lachaise after too many incidents of fans trying to unearth the former Doors vocalist.

For the past 58 years, a mysterious stranger has quietly slinked into the Baltimore cemetery where Edgar Allan Poe is buried and placed a bottle of French cognac and three roses on his grave.

Following DNA testing in 1998, the body of the "unknown soldier" of the Vietnam War was identified. In fact, thanks to advanced techniques, there will no longer be a need for such graves at Arlington National Cemetery.

When Kurt Cobain passed away, his widow, Courtney Love, had trouble finding a cemetery that would accept his remains, as all were fearful of the amount of vandalism that might occur at the site.

Serial killer Jeffrey Dahmer's brain wasn't cremated until 13 months after his death. Against his father's wishes, his mother had requested that it be studied for clues as to the reason behind his bizarre behavior.

Hair

Scotland, not Ireland, is home to a larger percentage of natural redheads (13 percent) than anywhere else on Earth.

First marketed in the 1970s, a shampoo known as Body on Tap was promoted as containing beer in every bottle.

While some spend hundreds to maintain their dreadlocks, the hair of African natives naturally grows in that style if left unattended.

Fueling rumors that his second son may not have been his, Prince Charles was reported to have said after first seeing newborn Harry: "Wherever did he get that rusty hair?"

Sportscaster Howard Cosell was shown to be bald after his hairpiece was plucked off his head during a segment on *ABC's Wide World of Sports* by the one man who could have gotten away with it: Muhammad Ali.

Blondes have more individual strands than other hair types, followed by brown, black, and red hair.

Cabbage Patch "Snacktime" Dolls were recalled in 1996 when it was discovered that, instead of gnawing on plastic vegetables, the dolls were sometimes chewing on (and pulling out) the hair of children.

Hawaii

There's only one royal palace in the United States; the Iolani Palace in Honolulu.

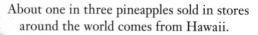

About one in three pineapples sold in stores around the world comes from Hawaii.

Pineapples aren't native to Hawaii; they were introduced to the Sandwich Islands (as Hawaii was then known) back in 1790.

The Hawaiian island of Oahu is home to the world's largest wind generator, with blades spanning a total of 400 feet atop a 20-story tower.

Hawaii is the only U.S. state whose border does not, at any point, form a straight line.

The world's first revolving restaurant was La Ronde, which opened in Hawaii's capital city in 1961.

In the nineteenth century, diseases brought to Hawaii by explorers from other nations reduced the native population from around 300,000 to less than 50,000.

Horses

The name of the palomino that played TV's *Mr. Ed* was Bamboo Harvester. The talented equine was said to be able to open doors, untie knots, and pick up a telephone.

Horses are physically unable to vomit.

To qualify as an official Budweiser horse, a Clydesdale must have four white stocking feet, a white blaze on his face, and a black mane and tail.

To avoid confusion with age limits in events, all thoroughbred race horses in the Northern Hemisphere are given an official birthday of January 1 of the year they were born.

The only U.S. survivor of the Battle of Little Bighorn was an Army horse named Comanche.

Miniature horses can be trained to be guide animals for the blind. They're particularly useful for sight-impaired persons who are allergic to (or afraid of) dogs.

The first U.S. mint in Philadelphia used harnessed horses to power the machine that produced the coins.

Hospitals & Health Care

While it's certainly rural, Plains, Georgia, is big enough to have a hospital. Jimmy Carter was born there, making him the first U.S. president ever to have been born in a hospital.

Dr. Daniel Hale Williams, who performed the first successful open-heart surgery in 1893, went on to open the first black-owned hospital in the United States three years later.

In Britain and Australia until the mid-nineteenth century, women who had contacted sexually transmitted diseases were placed into quarantined buildings known as *lock hospitals*.

Hospitals refer to the first 60 minutes after an injury or acute illness as the "golden hour." A patient's chances of survival are best when treated early in this time period.

The largest healthcare system in the United States is operated by the Department of Veterans Affairs, providing services for the nation's retired military personnel and their families.

Frank Marino of the band Mahogany Rush claimed that, while hospitalized to recover from a bad drug experience, the ghost of Jimi Hendrix visited him, suddenly enabling him to play rock guitar.

According to 2004 statistics, only three in four Texans are covered by health insurance, the lowest percentage in the nation.

Hot

Recent "global warming" hasn't proved hot enough to break the highest recorded temperature on Earth, set when the mercury peaked at 136° F. in Al 'Aziziyah, Libya, way back in 1922.

Mail-order pharmaceuticals can be a tricky business in the hot states of the American southwest. Some prescription drugs can lose up to 50 percent of their effectiveness after sitting in a hot mailbox all day.

In 1998, one manufacturer's historic automotive output surpassed two billion vehicles, more than the combined total of Ford, GM, and Chrysler. It was toy manufacturer Mattel, and the vehicles were Hot Wheels.

Research done in 2003 by Harvard Medical School shows that men who regularly eat hot whole-grain cereals (like oatmeal) lower their risk of cardiovascular disease by 17 percent.

The earliest home "hot tub" spas in the United States appeared in California in the 1960s, when they were makeshift affairs crafted using old vats from nearby wineries.

George M. Cohan's first hit song was "Hot Tamale Alley," written in 1901 when he was only 17 years of age.

What were called "soup-ups" in the 1930s gained a new name in the 1940s: hot rods.

Hotels

In the game of Monopoly, while you can "print" more money (by rule) if the bank runs out, you can *not* make more houses or hotels: the game is meant to have a limited number of each.

The Westminster Kennel Club was formed in 1877 when a group of dog fanciers founded the organization in the bar at the Westminster Hotel in Manhattan.

The motion picture *Grand Hotel* won the Best Picture Oscar at the Academy Awards ceremony on November 18, 1932. The following year, the event was moved to the spring.

In 2006, the 251 rooms of Washington's Watergate Hotel (the site of the celebrated 1973 break-in that led to Richard Nixon's resignation) were transformed into 96 "luxury residences."

The structure depicted on the cover of the Eagles' 1976 *Hotel California* album is on Sunset Boulevard; it's the Beverly Hills Hotel (a.k.a. "the Pink Palace").

The Maxwell House hotel in Nashville served a special blend of coffee that was so popular that it was first sold under the inn's name back in 1886.

In 1978, the Resorts Casino Hotel on the Boardwalk in Atlantic City became the site of the United States' first legal casino located outside the state of Nevada.

The Human Body

A healthy human being emits flatulence an average of five times a day, releasing approximately 17 ounces of intestinal gas.

While persons blind in one eye suffer from a complete lack of depth perception, they only lose about one-fifth of their total range of vision.

Human babies are born with around 300 bones, some of which fuse together. By the time we're adults, the number has decreased to 206.

Hair is made from the same substance as fingernails and toenails, so most substances that are beneficial to hair growth also help to make stronger, healthier nails.

Studies indicate that the rate of heart disease is lower in men who donate blood regularly when compared to those who do not.

Although estimates vary, human beings blink their eyes about five million times annually.

Your teeth chatter when you're cold because your facial muscles are quickly flexing in an effort to generate heat.

Independence Day

In 2002, about two thirds of the $7.9 million worth of American flags bought in the United States were made in China.

The U.S. Congress did not declare Independence Day a legal federal holiday until 1941.

Every Fourth of July, 50 swearing-in ceremonies for new U.S. citizens are coordinated nationwide. In recent years, more than half of those taking part in these events have been Latin Americans.

The world's one-minute rainfall record occurred on July 4, 1956, in Unionville, Maryland. Measurements indicated that 1.23 inches of rain fell in only 60 seconds.

In a letter to his wife, John Adams indicated that the new nation's most celebrated date would be July 2 (on which Congress officially declared independence), not July 4 (when they approved the text of the Declaration of Independence).

Celebratory Americans consume an estimated 150 million hot dogs on the Fourth of July.

In his patriot hit "Yankee Doodle Dandy," George M. Cohan claimed to be "born on the fourth of July." In fact, the songwriter was born on July 3, 1878.

Insects

While most related urban legends are untrue, cockroaches are known to be fond of the glue on stamps and envelopes, so it's best to keep these items in sealed containers.

Termites reportedly become frantic and eat through wood at a much more rapid pace when they're exposed to loud music.

Just as bees pollinate sweet-smelling plants, flies are attracted to (and pollinate) foul-smelling ones.

Entomologists estimate that about one in every four animals currently living on Earth is a beetle.

Mosquito repellants do not "repel" mosquitoes; rather, they make you invisible to the mosquitoes.

Every species of insect, without exception, has six legs.

The dragonfly is known by many different names in various regions of the United States. It may be a *darning needle*, an *ear sewer*, a *mosquito hawk*, or even a *snake feeder*.

The Internet

"Jerry's Guide to the World Wide Web" is still operating today, but under a much better-known name: Yahoo!

In 2000, the nation of Tuvalu signed a cool $50 million deal to lease out its ".TV" Internet domain extension for resale.

Researchers believe that 60 percent is a conservative estimate of the amount of e-mails sent that are unsolicited or "spam."

On March 15, 1985, symbolics.com became the first Internet domain name to be officially registered.

The rarely used @ sign was near elimination from the standard keyboard until 1971, when it was used in early computer code that became an integral part of e-mail communications.

In the mid-1990s, about half of the world's Internet users were from the United States. By the mid-2000s, this ratio had been cut to about one-fifth.

Inventions

Julius Schmid got the idea for his invention of the modern condom from his hours putting meat into casing at his job as a sausage maker.

The two-stick popsicle was introduced during the Great Depression to allow buyers to share the inexpensive treat with a friend.

Peter Durand patented the tin can in 1810, but it was 48 years later that Ezra Warner patented the first can opener.

New York housewife Joy Mangano wasn't satisfied with the millions she made from her Miracle Mop invention, so she followed that up by devising the popular Roly Kit.

John Stalberger invented the Hacky Sack in 1972 as a way to rehabilitate his knee, which he'd injured playing football.

Trying to develop a spring to stabilize submarine instruments, Richard James knocked one off a shelf and watched it "walk" down to a tabletop, inadvertently inventing the Slinky.

The mother of Michael Nesmith of the Monkees didn't have to depend on her son for income; she made millions after patenting the first liquid typing correction fluid.

In 1877, wanting to keep his telephone conversations private, Bell assistant Thomas Watson invented the first soundproof booth.

On August 4, 1922, telephone service in the United States and Canada was suspended for 60 seconds (at 6:25 P.M. Eastern) in tribute to inventor Alexander Graham Bell, who had passed away two days earlier.

The first use of the sideways "smile" emoticon :-) has been traced to a post made on a computer billboard dated September 19, 1982.

Jeans

In 1950, Levi Strauss brought canvas to San Francisco not to sew pants, but to make tents. Only after he arrived and was told how badly gold miners needed sturdy pants did he alter his plans.

While it lessened the sturdiness of the jeans, the rivets were eventually removed from the back pockets of Levis due to complaints that they were causing damage to chairs and sofas.

During the 1970s, a widely spread (but false) rumor hinted that eccentric musician Frank Zappa was the real-life son of Hugh 'Lumpy' Brannum, best known as Mr. Green Jeans on TV's *Captain Kangaroo*.

The "designer jean" craze kicked off in 1978 after the Nakash brothers launched the Jordache brand. J.C. Penney later fought the trend with unadorned "Plain Pockets" jeans.

Denim pants weren't commonly referred to as "jeans" until the 1960s. Before that, they were known as "waist overalls," "dungarees" or just "work pants."

The stitching design on the back pockets of Levi jeans is called an *arcuate*. It was originally there to hold the cotton lining of the pocket in place, but is now only used for decorative purposes.

What brand of jeans has been promoted by the likes of Anna Nicole Smith, Claudia Schiffer, and Drew Barrymore? Guess. No, that's the answer: Guess.

Jewelry & Gemstones

Diamonds were not a standard part of the engagement ring until DeBeers launched an aggressive advertising campaign in 1939.

Upon hearing the news of Princess Diana's death, one of Queen Elizabeth's first duties was to see to the safe return of any Royal jewelry that the princess was wearing.

In the book *The Wonderful Wizard of Oz*, the slippers worn by Dorothy were made not of rubies, but of silver.

Opal (the birthstone for October) contains a higher percentage of water (up to 10 percent) than most stones, meaning that it can easily be damaged if not handled carefully.

Richard Burton's first jewelry purchase for his then-wife Elizabeth Taylor was a 33.19 carat diamond ring, which Liz still wears today.

By definition, *sterling* silver must be made with 92.5 percent silver, and the rest copper. *Fine* silver is even more pure, 99.9 percent silver, but is generally too soft to be used in jewelry.

In the 1963 film (and its 2006 remake), the Pink Panther was neither a cartoon character nor a colorful feline, but a rare jewel.

Kangaroos

The Eastern Grey kangaroo is the largest marsupial in the world. It may reach 200 lbs in weight and 8 feet in height.

In the wild, kangaroos rarely live past six or seven years of age, but those in captivity may live three times as long.

With a 44 share, the 1964 episode of *The Beverly Hillbillies* in which the family mistakes a kangaroo for a giant jackrabbit is the highest-rated half-hour TV show ever.

Kangaroos live in groups known as "mobs" that may have only a few members or as many as 100.

Thanks to the elimination of its most dangerous predator (the Tasmanian wolf), the kangaroo population has grown in Australia, and is thought to be higher than ever before.

Female kangaroos are often in a perpetual state of motherhood, becoming pregnant only days after giving birth. They have the interesting capability to "pause" the development of the embryo inside them, however, until the existing joey leaves the pouch.

Like cows, kangaroos have chambered stomachs, and some species regurgitate "cud" and chew it again to aid in digestion.

Kitchen Appliances

The first practical dishwasher was invented by socialite Josephine Cochran in 1893. Her servants had become careless with her fine china, and she didn't want to wash the dishes herself.

Around 75 million George Foreman grills have been sold worldwide since the appliances were first marketed in 1995.

The first food intentionally cooked by microwave power was popcorn. Having seen the effect of the waves on a candy bar in his pocket, Dr. Percy Spencer placed popcorn kernels in front of a magnetron and watched them pop.

The technology that led to the refrigerator was first developed by a Florida doctor in 1834 to lower the temperatures of patients afflicted with yellow fever.

The electric toaster was invented in 1905, more than 25 years before sliced bread became available at retail stores.

Trying to make kitchen cleanup easier for his wife, John Hammes invented the garbage disposal in 1927. He named the device the "Electric Pig."

The first microwave oven sold for commercial use was as tall as a human adult and five times as heavy.

Law Enforcement

The name "bobby" used to refer to London police-men goes back to Robert Peel, who organized the city's Metropolitan Police force.

In addition to ammunition and body armor, most police cruisers carry stuffed animals in their trunks as well, to soothe frightened children encountered on the job.

The first sworn female police officer in the United States, Alice Stebbins Wells of Los Angeles, had to design and sew her own uniform when she began serving in 1910.

Many police departments prefer to use European-bred dogs, consider-ing them better for duty. Confiscated drug money is sometimes used to defray the cost of acquiring these canines.

At his home in Weybridge in 1967, John Lennon was intrigued by the sound of a distant police siren. He incorporated a similar wail into the Beatles song "I Am the Walrus."

The first "pony car" to be used by a major law enforcement organization was the 1971 AMC Javelin. One hundred thirty-three of these models were used by the Alabama State Police for patrol and pursuit duties.

When he passed away in 1982, Jack Webb (star of *Dragnet*) became the first civilian in Los Angeles to be buried with full police honors. His badge number, 714, was also retired.

Legal Trivia

In American courtrooms, John Doe is the name used for an anonymous defendant. An unknown plaintiff, on the other hand, is referred to as Richard Roe.

The restrictions on those "do not remove under penalty of law" mattress tags don't apply to the owner, but to the retailer.

We have Ernesto Miranda to thank for our "Miranda rights." The Arizona native was interrogated (and ultimately convicted) without knowing he had the option of legal representation.

For many years, thanks to the efforts of dairy farmers who wanted to keep their customers, it was illegal for margarine makers to color their product yellow.

The nationwide program known as an "Amber Alert" is named after Amber Hagerman, a nine-year-old abducted in Texas in 1996.

Celebrated attorney Clarence Darrow only completed a single year of law school.

The term "palimony" was coined in 1976 when Michelle Triola unsuccessfully sued actor Lee Marvin, with whom she had lived for seven years, for one-half of his assets.

Letters & Numbers

Four is the only number in the English language in which the number of letters matches the value.

Coincidentally, it takes 52 letters to spell out all the values (Ace, Two, Three, etc.) in a regular deck of 52 playing cards.

Only one letter of the alphabet doesn't appear in any atomic symbol in the Periodic Table: it's *J*.

The inventor of Scrabble based each letter's point value on the average frequency of their appearance on the front page of several editions of *The New York Times*.

If you were to arrange all the whole numbers alphabetically, the first on the list would be "eight," and the last would be "zero."

Only four capital letters in the English alphabet appear the same if seen upside down and/or in a mirror: H, I, O, and X.

Literature

Mary Shelley was only 19 years old when she wrote the classic novel *Frankenstein* on a dare from poet (and friend) Lord Byron over who could write the most frightening tale.

Drummer Joey Kramer suggested the name Aerosmith shortly after the rock group had formed, but his band mates vetoed it at first, because it reminded them of the Sinclair Lewis novel *Arrowsmith* that they'd been forced to read in high school.

Stephen Crane managed to conjure up vivid battle scenes in his Civil War novel *The Red Badge of Courage* despite the fact that he'd never served in the military or ever saw live combat.

Dean Koontz turned "professional" much earlier than most writers; at the age of eight, he typed up short stories and sold them to his neighbors for five cents each.

Acclaimed novelist Norman Mailer threw his hat into the ring in 1960 for the New York City mayoral race, but ruined his chances for political glory when he stabbed his wife with a pair of scissors after a drunken celebration.

Lolita author Vladimir Nabokov was also a noted lepidopterist. He discovered and named several new species of butterflies, and organized the collection at Harvard University's Museum of Comparative Zoology.

At a towering 6'9" in height, prolific author Michael Crichton is three inches taller than basketball legend Michael Jordan.

Losers

The Detroit Lions are the oldest existing NFL franchise to have never appeared in the Super Bowl.

George H. W. Bush has been the only U.S. president over the last 25 years to fail in his bid for reelection.

Per Jewish tradition, there's a distinct difference between a *schlemiel* and a *schlimazel.* The former is one who spills his soup; the latter is the person on whom the soup is spilled.

In addition to having an unfortunate last name, the *Li'l Abner* character known as Joe Btfsplk was so down-and-out that a storm cloud always hovered over his head.

Among the faux taxonomic names for Wile E. Coyote have been:

Appetitus giganticus
Caninus nervous rex
Carnivorous slobbius
Eatius birdius
Famishus fantasticus
Hardheadipus Oedipus
Road-Runnerus digestus

Made in Japan

Before 1982, cars bearing Japanese nameplates were nearly all made in Japan. That year, Honda opened their first U.S. plant in Ohio, opening the floodgates for all others.

A JVC VHS VCR? That translates to a Japan Victor Company Video Home System (format) Video Cassette Recorder. JVC introduced the VHS format to compete with Sony's Beta setup back in 1976.

While it's more commonly associated with Chinese food, monosodium glutamate (MSG) was developed in 1908 in Japan.

While Nintendo became better known for their video games, the Japanese company was founded in 1898 as a manufacturer of playing cards.

The Japanese word "banzai" literally means "(may you live) 10 thousand years."

The 1989 motion picture *The Adventures of Milo and Otis* was originally filmed for Japanese television. Dudley Moore added narration to the story before its theatrical release in America.

The best-selling automobile model in the history of the world is the Toyota Corolla, with more than 30 million sold since the first one rolled off the assembly line in 1966.

Magazines

For the first 33 years of publication (until 1955), *Reader's Digest* was missing something found in nearly every other magazine: advertisements.

"Relax" hit makers Frankie Goes to Hollywood got their name from a headline of an old issue of *Variety* magazine.

Edgar Allan Poe's *The Murders in the Rue Morgue*, widely considered the world's first detective story, was first published in *Graham's* magazine.

In 2003, *mental_floss* magazine's "Swimsuit Issue" featured undoctored beachwear photos of several well-known historical figures, including Eleanor Roosevelt and Albert Einstein.

The average American household subscribes to or purchases six different magazines a year.

Suffering from a ruptured appendix, a young Donny Osmond was nevertheless pushed to finish a photo shoot for *16* magazine, which he did before leaving for the hospital.

Dr. Hook & the Medicine Show, the band who scored a hit with "The Cover of the Rolling Stone," finally did appear on front of the magazine on March 29, 1973.

Medicine

While cows can get cowpox, chickenpox has nothing to do with poultry; the disease was so named because it was weaker than smallpox.

The first successful cesarean section (after which both mother and newborn survived) was performed in 1500 by a Swiss pig gelder on his wife.

"Doc" Holliday was a notorious alcoholic, gambler, and gunslinger. But he *was* a real doctor (or more accurately, a dentist).

The term "quack" to describe an incompetent doctor comes from *quacksalver*, the name given to nineteenth-century con artists who sold phony "healing" potions and ointments.

Be glad you weren't practicing medicine during the seventeenth century—in those days, doctors tested patients for diabetes by tasting their urine. The amount of sugar detected was the telling sign.

That aroma that makes all dentists' offices smell alike comes from *clove oil*, which is an ingredient in the topical anesthetic used by most tooth doctors.

Until the mid-1700s, barbers in England were also surgeons. They not only removed unruly hair, but also teeth, kidney stones, and the occasional gangrenous leg.

Medicine Cabinet Items

The cotton swabs now known as Q-Tips were christened Baby Gays by their inventor, Leo Gerstenzang.

The phrase "Always a bridesmaid, never a bride" was introduced in a 1923 advertisement for Listerine mouthwash.

Viagra was originally clinically tested as a heart medicine. Its "other" properties were unknown until the male test subjects refused to return their unused pills at the end of the trial period.

In addition to acting and providing the voice of Tigger for *Winnie the Pooh*, Paul Winchell also patented one of the first disposable razor designs.

When Flintstones Vitamins first added Betty to the mix in 1996, they removed one shape—the Stone Age car—to make room.

Before she joined TV's *Charlie's Angels*, Shelley Hack appeared in several commercials promoting a popular perfume, coincidentally named Charlie.

Men vs. Women

Red-green colorblindness, also known as *dichromatism*, is seven times more common in men than it is in women.

The average male human brain weighs about five ounces more than the average female's brain.

While Alaska is no longer the male-dominated frontier once advertised, it still has the highest male-to-female ratio (107:100) of any U.S. state.

By contrast, Rhode Island is "where the women are." There are fewer than 93 males for every 100 females in the Ocean State.

The state with the closest balance amongst the sexes is Arizona, with a nearly identical number of men and women amongst its 5-million-plus population.

Helen Reddy co-wrote the #1 hit "I Am Woman" with an Australian composer who was not of the female persuasion. His name is Ray Burton.

Stella Walsh of Poland won the women's 100-meter race at the 1932 Olympic Games. It wasn't until she died in 1980 that an autopsy revealed she was actually a man.

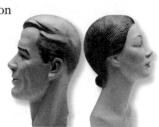

Military Schools

Just as our nation's gold supply is housed at Fort Knox, the United States' silver is stored at another military facility: the U.S. Military Academy at West Point.

Shannon Faulkner, who sued the Citadel to allow her entry in 1993 as the first woman in the military college, dropped out after only six days.

Colorado Springs was selected as the site of the Air Force Academy only after Charles Lindbergh took committee members on a flight over the area and proclaimed it suitable.

When West Point opened in 1802, the curriculum was centered on drafting, math, and military fortification. Many of the students did not know how to read or write.

Physical Education is an integral part of training at the Naval Academy in Annapolis; each student is trained in boxing, judo, swimming, wrestling, and personal conditioning.

New York State is home to not only the Military Academy at West Point, but also the Merchant Marine Academy in Kings Point.

Milk & Milk Cows

A cow must have given birth before she will begin to give milk, and most cows are artificially impregnated once a year to keep the milk flowing.

Studies have shown that milk and other dairy products are better for the bones than are calcium supplements.

It takes more than 20 lbs. of milk to produce one pound of butter, but only about half as much to make one pound of cheese or ice cream.

Reduced-fat milk, at 2 percent, contains between one half and two thirds as much fat as whole milk, which is 3.5 percent fat.

On average, a cow's udder must be squeezed around 350 times to give one gallon of fresh milk.

Thanks to genetic improvements and technological advances, today's cows may provide 10 gallons of milk per day, several times the natural amount.

Geneticists are attempting to develop cows that will produce milk more easily tolerated by the billions of lactose-intolerant persons on Earth.

Miscellaneous

The Pony Express went under after a little over a year of operation. The invention of the telegraph made the speedy mail service obsolete.

If today is your birthday, you're one of nearly 18 million persons worldwide to turn one year older.

During their trek to the Pacific, the Lewis & Clark party sometimes had to subsist on less-than-desirable food, which occasionally included dog meat.

Chevy Chase is more than just the name of a comedic actor; it's also the name of a suburb of Washington, D.C.

In the last 25 years, more rabies cases in the United States have been traced to bat bites than to any other source.

Some 90 percent of the coal burned in the United States annually is used to make electricity.

In parts of Greece and other European nations, giving the "thumbs up" sign is considered a rude gesture akin to "flipping the bird."

In the Middle Ages, a hole was shaved on the top of the heads of Catholic priests, making it appear as if they had bald spots. (The beanie-like "zucchetto" hat worn today is a remnant of this procedure.)

In 1983, some 106 million viewers (half the U.S. population at the time) watched the final episode of *M*A*S*H*. The following year, only 92 million turned up to vote in the presidential election.

As of 2006, only one location in the United States is not subject to any law concerning the licensing of tattoo artists and tattooing equipment: Washington, D.C.

It takes from 7 to 15 minutes for the average human to fall asleep.

Elwood Edwards's voice is heard more than 50 million times on an average day. He's the man behind the "You've got mail!" voice on America Online.

A broken clock is right at least twice a day, whereas a working clock that loses one minute every day is accurate only once every two years.

In 1995, Bill Clinton was quoted as saying that the spork (the combination spoon-and-fork commonly seen at KFC restaurants) was "the symbol of [his] administration."

"Christmas Snow" is more than a yuletide wish; it was the proper name of Suzanne Somers's character on TV's *Three's Company*.

The tie-dye process popularized in the 1960s was originally devised in ancient China.

Misters

Only one member of The Byrds actually played a musical instrument on the band's hit version of "Mr. Tambourine Man"—Roger McGuinn played a Rickenbacker guitar.

If you're brave enough, feel free to call Mr. T by his real first name: Lawrence.

A 1980 Mr. PiBB soft drink contest sought the woman whose facial features most closely matched the "dream girl" an artist had envisioned. It was cancelled after ethnic groups complained that the woman depicted was Caucasian, giving them no chance to win.

The earliest Mr. Potato Head packages from the 1950s included many of the same facial features included in today's version, but not the plastic potato body. Kids then were expected to use a real potato.

After Mr. Mister broke up in 1989, lead vocalist Richard Page rejected offers to become a member of not one, but two other popular bands: Chicago and Toto.

Yankees catcher Thurman Munson first called Reggie Jackson "Mr. October" to mock how poorly he had performed in the 1977 AL Championship Series. Jackson turned the tables with a stellar performance in that year's World Series.

He's known in Italy as Mastro Lindo, in Spain as Don Limpio, and in Germany as Meister Proper. In the United States, he's known as Mr. Clean.

The Moon

What was once referred to as the "dark side" of the moon is more properly called the "far side." Although we cannot see the other side of the moon, it receives just as much sunlight as any other part of the lunar surface.

Some of the moon's craters would be massive even on Earth, measuring 150 miles in diameter.

The plaque placed on the moon by the first two men to land there was inscribed with not only their names, but the names of two others: then-President Nixon, and astronaut Michael Collins (who manned the capsule orbiting the moon).

The Craters of the Moon National Monument isn't on the lunar surface, but in Idaho.

While the moon is the largest object in the sky when seen from earth, it isn't even the biggest natural satellite in the solar system. That honor goes to Ganymede, one of Jupiter's moons.

Astronomers now believe the moon may be home to as much as 25 billion gallons of water in the form of ice, hiding in the shadows caused by craters on the surface.

The first two moon landings occurred in two seemingly opposite locations: the Sea of Tranquility and the Ocean of Storms.

The "Most"

Among the most commonly stolen items from drugstores are batteries, cosmetics, camera film, and Preparation H.

In 1993, squirrels overtook dogs as the most frequent victims of "hit-and-run" automobile drivers in the United States.

The song that was played the most number of times on American radio during the twentieth century was "You've Lost That Loving Feeling."

The record for the most appearances on the cover of *People* magazine belongs to Princess Diana, who had been pictured there a whopping 52 times through the year 2004.

Charged with crimes including burglary and murder, Donald Eugene Webb of Oklahoma has appeared on the FBI's 10 Most Wanted list since 1981, longer than any other person since the first such list was issued in 1950.

Until its removal in 2000, the most remote public telephone booth in the United States was believed to have been one located in the Mojave Desert, 75 miles southwest of Las Vegas, and 15 miles from the nearest road.

According to a 2005 study done by the University of Cardiff, the most depressing day of the year is January 24.

A Mother-Load of Trivia

Eric Clapton, Jack Nicholson, and Bobby Darin each grew up thinking their mothers were really their sisters.

Medical journals indicate that five-year-old Lina Medina of Peru became the world's youngest mother when she gave birth to a healthy baby in 1939.

Marie Osmond uses her middle name professionally. Her real first name is Olive, the same as her late mother's.

2003 Harvard research indicates that mothers pregnant with boys eat more food than those carrying girls.

The sweaters that children's TV host Fred Rogers wore on his show were all hand-knitted by his mother.

The late Roxie Roker, who portrayed Helen Willis on *The Jeffersons*, is mother to rocker Lenny Kravitz.

The average age for a first-time mother in the United States is now 25, higher than it's ever been.

Movie Tech Trivia

The last shot of the day on a movie set is called the "Martini shot"—presumably because the next "shot" that will be had will be part of a cocktail.

The name of the motion picture near the top of a promotional poster is called the "art title." It is a point of prestige for an actor to have his or her name above the art title.

If you're approached by a feature film-maker to use your home in a motion picture, you can expect to be compensated in the neighborhood of $1000 to $5000 per day

George Lucas was fined $250,000 by the Director's Guild for not listing any opening credits in his 1977 film *Star Wars*.

For many years in Hollywood, directors who wished to disassociate themselves from a particular film would credit themselves using the name Alan Smithee.

If you've wondered about the details of those "odd jobs" that you see in the credits of motion pictures, here's a short list:

The *gaffer* is the chief electrician on a movie set.

The *best boy* is key assistant to the gaffer.

The *key grip* supervises the placement and moving of lights, scenery, and cranes.

Movie Trivia

The 1974 film *Son of Dracula* included appearances by three of classic rock's best-known drummers: John Bonham (Led Zeppelin), Keith Moon (The Who), and Ringo Starr (The Beatles).

It's true: in the chariot scene of 1959's *Ben-Hur*, one of the characters (a trumpeter) can be seen wearing a wristwatch.

For years, extras in movies were instructed to repeat "Walla Walla" when appearing in crowd scenes, in order to keep from clashing with other dialogue.

Nearly all the action in the film *Fargo* didn't take place in North Dakota, but in Minnesota. And despite the disclaimer at the beginning of the film, it was not based on a true story.

Froggy, the deep-voiced, bespectacled character from the Our Gang comedy film shorts, had fewer birthdays than most people: he was born on February 29.

If you've wondered about the voice behind the vast majority of movie trailers over the last 30 years, wonder no longer: his name is Don LaFontaine.

The first winner of the Worst Film "Razzie" award was 1980's *Can't Stop the Music*, starring the one-two punch of Steve Guttenberg and the Village People.

Silver screen lover Rudolph Valentino lived up to his lover-boy image; he was arrested for bigamy in 1922.

Mushrooms

In ancient Egypt more than 4500 years ago, mushrooms were considered a delicacy fit only for royalty. Commoners weren't even allowed to touch them.

More than half of all the mushrooms cultivated in the United States are grown in Pennsylvania.

Using special techniques to produce imitation oak logs onto which shiitake mushrooms would grow, farmers have reduced harvest time from six years to only four months.

When rock band Heart left them for a new label in the middle of recording the album *Magazine*, Mushroom Records released their own version of the LP (with early mixes and some live tracks added) before being ordered by a judge to recall the discs.

The "stalk" of a mushroom that supports the cap is more properly called the "stipe."

Green bean casserole, a recipe that has long appeared on cans of Campbell's cream of mushroom soup, is considered the most popular "label" recipe ever published.

Two of the more frightening-sounding (and most poisonous) varieties of mushroom known to man include the Death Cap and the Destroying Angel.

Musical Instruments

The only discernible difference between a "fiddle" and a "violin" is the type of music being played by the instrument. Otherwise, they're exactly the same.

While his typical setup is much less expansive, Chad Smith of the Red Hot Chili Peppers once set a record for playing on a drum kit containing some 308 pieces.

The banjo has long been a favorite instrument of comedians. Those proficient on the instrument include Jerry Van Dyke and Steve Martin.

Bugles aren't limited to the army. Navies have long made use of the brass instruments too, since the shrill sound can be heard even in the roughest weather.

Better known in the United States for their motorcycles, Yamaha has only been making them since 1955. They've produced pianos, by contrast, for nearly 220 years.

The piano covers the full musical range of an orchestra. It can hit notes lower than a bassoon and higher than a piccolo.

In addition to the saxophone, Belgian inventor Adolphe Sax also devised other instruments, including the saxhorn and the saxotromba.

Whenever he's in town and available, Woody Allen plays clarinet with a jazz band every Monday evening at The Carlyle (formerly Michael's Pub) on Madison Avenue in New York.

Musical Manson

Both The Beach Boys and Guns 'n Roses recorded songs written by Charles Manson.

Contrary to rumor, Charles Manson never auditioned for The Monkees; he was imprisoned at the time the tryouts were being held.

Music producer Terry Melcher (who also happened to be Doris Day's son) had shown interest in recording Manson's first album, though no deal ever occurred.

Noted gangster Alvin 'Creepy' Karpis befriended 'Little Charlie' Manson in prison in the early 1960s and taught him to play the guitar.

Several members of the Manson Family (including Charlie) lived for a while in a home owned by The Beach Boys' Dennis Wilson.

Charles Manson thought The Beatles' song "Helter Skelter" was about Armageddon; in fact, the title is just a British term for a playground slide.

Although Charlie didn't appear on the record, several remaining members of the Manson Family released a 1970 album filled with their renditions of 13 songs he had written.

Musical Plagiarism

The opening lyrical line in The Beatles' song "Come Together" was taken from Chuck Berry's "You Can't Catch Me."

John Fogerty's single "Old Man Down the Road" was the subject of a lawsuit by the copyright owners of an earlier recording on which Fogerty also sang, the Creedence Clearwater Revival hit "Run Through the Jungle."

Two 1980s hit makers squared off in court when it was asserted that Ray Parker Jr.'s theme song for the film *Ghostbusters* was a rip-off of the Huey Lewis & the News song "I Want a New Drug."

A judge found the Andrews Sisters' recording of "Rum and Coca-Cola" to be too similar to an earlier calypso recording, awarding damages to the plaintiff. The defendants included comedian Morey Amsterdam (who penned the words to the song).

Ira Arnstein launched a succession of five lawsuits against persons he felt were plagiarizing his works. They finally ended when he lost his case against the legendary songwriter Cole Porter.

One key element helped Britney Spears win a 2003 lawsuit over her song "What U See is What U Get": the plaintiffs could not prove that Spears or the credited songwriters had ever heard their similarly titled recording.

ZZ Top sued Chrysler over the music in a Plymouth Prowler ad, which resembled their song "La Grange." Chrysler argued that the song's guitar riff had appeared on earlier songs (including Norman Greenbaum's "Spirit in the Sky").

Name Changes

Despite his surly demeanor, Ulysses S. Grant was born with the touchy-feely initials H. U. G.; he was born Hiram Ulysses Grant.

In early drafts of *Gone with the Wind*, Margaret Mitchell's lead character was named Pansy instead of Scarlett.

Charles Dickens considered the names Little Larry and Puny Pete for the character that ended up being called Tiny Tim in *A Christmas Carol*.

Winnie the Pooh is actually the famous bear's nickname; his proper name is Edward.

Iron Eyes Cody, the tearful "Native American" in the famous PSA about pollution, was born with a different name (and nationality). He was actually an Italian-American named Espera DeCorti.

In the first television pilot for *All in the Family*, Archie and the members of his family had a different last name: Justice.

Born David Jones, the songster who became David Bowie was forced to change his name to avoid confusion with another British-born singer who was a member of The Monkees.

Marilyn Monroe's last name at birth wasn't Baker, as commonly believed, but Mortensen.

Names in the News

"Baby Jessica" McClure, who was rescued from a Texas well after 58 hours in 1987, has grown up. As of 2006, the newly married 19-year-old attended Midland College.

Michael Fay, the 18-year-old American who was arrested and sentenced to a caning for vandalizing cars in Singapore, was last heard from in 1998, when he was arrested in Florida for possession of marijuana.

Six-year-old refugee Eliàn Gonzàlez was the subject of an international custody battle when he was found floating on an inner tube in 1999. Today, Eliàn is back in his native Cuba, where he told *60 Minutes* that he considers Fidel Castro a "friend and a father."

The world breathed a sigh of relief in 2002 when the nine trapped men in Pennsylvania's Quecreek

Mine were rescued after three days. Of the rescued, only Randy Fogle still works underground at the Quecreek Mine.

AP correspondent Terry Anderson was kidnapped in 1985 and held hostage in Beirut for seven years before his release. Remembering his days of starvation, he's opened two restaurants, a delicatessen, and an international food import/export business.

William Figueroa (age 12) toured the talk show circuit after correcting then-Vice President Dan Quayle on the proper spelling of "potato." Figueroa dropped out of school five years later and (as of 2006) worked as a department manager at a Wal-Mart store.

Darva Conger made headlines as the "winner" of TV's *Who Wants to Marry a Millionaire* in 2000. After the marriage was annulled, she posed for *Playboy*, married a paramedic, and hosted a short-lived TV series called *Vegas Weddings Unveiled*.

National Anthems

The first letters of the 15 stanzas of the Netherlands' national anthem form an acrostic that spells out "Willem van Nassov" (William of Orange).

"The Bonnie Blue Flag" was the name of the national anthem of the Confederate States of America. It was sung to the tune of an existing melody titled "The Irish Jaunting Cart."

The opening notes of The Beatles' hit "All You Need Is Love" come directly from France's national anthem, *"Le Marseillaise."*

Officially, the Spanish national anthem has no lyrics.

In 1813, two years after Johann Rudolf Wyss wrote the lyrics for the national anthem of Switzerland, he published his most famous novel: *The Swiss Family Robinson.*

The Liechtenstein national anthem, "Oben am jungen Rhein," has a melody familiar to Britons. It uses the same exact tune as "God Save the Queen."

"The Star-Spangled Banner" was 117 years old when Congress finally passed a bill making it the national anthem of the United States in 1931.

Natural Disasters

A near-100-foot wave crashes into a cruise ship? It sounds like *The Poseidon Adventure* circa 1970, but it's actually the *Queen Elizabeth II* in 1995. The massive water rush from off Newfoundland's coast caused only minor damage.

In the past half-century, Florida has experienced twice as many tornadoes as Illinois, but those Sunshine State twisters have caused only half as many deaths as the ones in the Land of Lincoln.

The fire triggered by the 1906 San Francisco earthquake caused several times more damage than the tremor itself.

In an average year, more Americans are killed by flash floods than by hurricanes, tornadoes, or any other type of weather-related event.

The new millennium has seen both ends of the storm spectrum. While 2005 was a record year for hurricanes in the United States, not a single one made landfall in the States in 2000.

About 90 percent of the active volcanoes in the world are located in lands along the Pacific Ocean, known as the "ring of fire." In the United States, you'll find them in Hawaii, Alaska, Washington, Oregon, and California.

NHL hockey teams named for natural disasters are the Carolina Hurricanes and the Colorado Avalanche. Of course, the Tampa Bay Lightning might also cause a fire.

New Year's Eve & Day

One hundred lights adorned the first "ball" dropped in Times Square on New Year's Eve, back in 1907.

The Muslim calendar has only 354 days, so each year comes more quickly. In 2008, Muslims will celebrate New Year's Day on January 10 and again on December 29.

In 2000, the Times Square "ball" was given a name: the Star of Hope.

Different areas of the world enjoy different foods to celebrate the New Year. In Vietnam, it's watermelon; in Italy, it's pork; in Poland, it's pickled herring.

According to Hallmark, the dead of winter is "party time." New Year's Eve is the biggest day for parties, followed by Super Bowl Sunday.

One third of all fireworks injuries that occur on New Year's Eve and other holidays in the United States are due to illegal fireworks, notably M80 and M100 explosives.

Until 1752, America (and all other British colonies) celebrated New Year's Day on March 25 instead of January 1.

Newborns

Emilio Palma was born farther south than any other human, at a research base in Antarctica in 1978.

The original model for the Gerber baby was Ann Turner Cook, not Humphrey Bogart as widely rumored.

Mark your calendar: little James Tiberius Kirk (of *Star Trek*) will be born on March 22, 2238, in the town of Riverside, Iowa.

Infants are born with rudimentary kneecaps that don't fully begin to form until between three and six years of age.

Louise Brown, the world's first test-tube baby, now makes "deliveries" of her own as a postal worker in her hometown of Bristol, England.

Days-old, prematurely born babies are used in Hollywood productions to fill the role of brand-newborns. Cream cheese and red jelly is applied to their bodies to complete the "look."

In February 2006, a 37-lb. California woman gave birth to a healthy baby via C-section.

Newspapers

The largest-circulation newspaper in the United States isn't published in New York or Washington, but in McLean, Virginia. That's the home office of *USA Today*.

Newspaper wire services often use the abbreviation POTUS to save ink; the acronym stands for President of the United States.

In at least one of the *Superman* storylines, reporter Clark Kent receives a Pulitzer Prize for his work with *The Daily Planet*.

Historians consider the first newspaper comic strip to be Richard Outcault's *Hogan's Alley*. It spawned a popular character known as the Yellow Kid.

In 1846, the *London Daily News* hired its first editor, whose abilities as a writer were well-known: Charles Dickens.

The original "Ask Ann Landers" column was written by a nurse at the *Chicago Sun-Times* who spent most of her time answering readers' medical questions.

Per a 2004 study, the most-read sections of newspapers in the United States begin with main news, followed by local news, entertainment, sports, and comics.

Office Machinery

Benjamin Hotchkiss not only invented the stapler, but also the modern machine gun. In some countries, "Hotchkiss" is still used as a generic name for a stapler.

The QWERTY keyboard still commonly used today was initially developed to divide common letter pairs between the hands. This kept the keys on old manual typewriters from jamming when used by speedy typists.

The first facsimile machine was patented in 1843, some 30 years before the telephone. Early faxes were sent via telegraph.

Manila envelopes were named after Manila hemp, a type of fiber native to the Philippines that is used in the production of various paper products.

Physicist Chet Carlson, frustrated with the speed of Photostat machines, developed xerography back in 1938. It took seven years for a company to agree to produce and market his new copy machines.

Art Fry took an adhesive invented by a 3M colleague and applied it to some paper to make a bookmark for his songbook at church. He then took the idea one step further and invented Post-It Notes.

The red Swingline stapler that was a key prop in the film *Office Space* was specially made for the movie. Only after they'd received scores of requests did the company finally market its own red stapler.

The Olympic Games

Only two nations, Australia and Greece, have participated in each of the modern Olympic Games.

Princess Anne of Britain was the only participant in the 1976 Summer Olympics not subjected to a medical test to verify her sex.

Medal winners were responsible for 77 deaths at the 1900 Olympics … the victims were pigeons, unwilling participants in a live pigeon shooting event.

Despite hosting the Winter Olympics twice (in 1932 and 1980), the tiny town of Lake Placid, NY, is home to only about 2,500 residents.

As the human body in competition was then considered a thing of beauty, athletes at the ancient Olympics participated in their events in the nude.

At the first modern Olympics in 1896, more than two thirds of the participants were Greek.

Only one Summer Olympic event involved a powered craft: motor boating. Three races were part of the 1908 Games, after which the sport was dropped from the program.

On the Job

The "office structure" as we know it today (directors, branches, management, employees) was developed by the railroads, which were too spread out to be controlled locally. As they went national, banks and insurance companies followed suit.

Per the most recent data, about one in four on-the-job fatalities occurs when the employee is operating a company automobile.

The word "salary" is derived from the Latin *salarium*, meaning a payment made in salt. (Salt was a valuable commodity in medieval times.)

The Blue Cross organization started out in 1929 as a hospital pre-payment plan for schoolteachers in Dallas, Texas.

From the Civil War until the Great Depression (when Social Security began), the only pensions given to the elderly were awarded to veterans and their widows.

Over the last 50 years, the number of private-sector workers who are union members has decreased from more than one third to less than 10 percent.

Henry Ford introduced the 40-hour workweek in 1926. He felt that giving employees additional leisure time would give them more time to shop and travel, helping the economy.

One-Word Titles

Not every song title is book-length. Following is a list of all the one-word pop song titles that hit #1 in the rock era (from 1955 to 2005). How many of these recordings do you remember?

"ABC"	"Abracadabra"	"Africa"
"Again"	"Alone"	"Always"
"Amanda"	"Amazed"	"Angel"
"Angie"	"Babe"	"Bad"
"Bailamos"	"Batdance"	"Believe"
"Ben"	"Bent"	"Bootylicious"
"Burn"	"Butterfly"	"Calcutta"
"Celebration"	"Centerfold"	"Cherish"
"Convoy"	"Cream"	"Creep"
"Dilemma"	"Dizzy"	"Dominique"
"Don't"	"Downtown"	"Dreamlover"
"Dreams"	"Emotions"	"Escapade"
"Faith"	"Fallin'"	"Fame"
"Fantasy"	"Fire"	"Foolish"
"Footloose"	"Frankenstein"	"Ghostbusters"
"Goodies"	"Grease"	"Groovin'"

"Heartbreaker"

"Heaven"	"Hello"
"Help!"	"Hero"

"Honey"   "Honeycomb"   "Human"
"Hypnotize"   "Incomplete"   "Informer"
"Joyride"   "Jump"   "Kiss"
"Kokomo"   "Kyrie"   "Lady"
"Lately"   "Magic"   "Mandy"
"Maneater"   "Maniac"   "Medley"
"Michael"   "Mickey"   "MMMbop"
"Monkey"   "Music"   "Patricia"
"Photograph"   "Physical"   "Rapture"
"Respect"   "Reunited"   "Ringo"
"Rise"   "Romantic"   "Runaway"
"Sailing"   "Sara"   "Satisfied"
"Shakedown"   "Sheila"   "Sherry"
"Shout"   "Sincerely"   "Sledgehammer"
"Smooth"   "Someday"   "Stay"
"Still"   "Stutter"   "Sukiyaki"
"Sundown"   "Superstition"   "Surrender"
"Sussudio"   "Tammy"   "Telstar"
"Tequila"   "Tragedy"   "Truly"
"Unbelievable"   "Unpretty"   "Venus"
"Vogue"   "Wannabe"   "War"
"Waterfalls"   "Weak"   "Why"
"Windy"   "Yeah!"   "Yesterday"

Onomatopoeia

In English, the bark of a dog is written using imitative sounds, most commonly "woof-woof," "arf-arf," and "bow-wow." Other languages use different representations of the same noise. Following is a partial list of some of our favorites:

Language	Sound
Czech	haf-haf
Dutch	woef-woef
French	woah-woah
German	wau-wau
Greek	gav-gav
Hindi	bho-bho
Indonesian	gong-gong
Italian	bau-bau
Japanese	wan-wan
Korean	mung-mung
Norwegian	vof-vof
Polish	hau-hau
Portuguese	au-au
Spanish	guau-guau
Swedish	vov-vov
Turkish	hev-hev

Owls

Owls can turn their heads three quarters of the way around.

Nursing pioneer Florence Nightingale had an owl named Athena that she often kept in her pocket.

An owl has 14 vertebrae in its neck, twice as many as humans.

A hungry owl will eat its prey whole and then cough up the indigestible leftovers.

An owl's eyes are fixated straight ahead due to bony plates in the skull; that's why it must move its head to see.

Seven owls, named Bandit, Elmo, Gizmo, Kasper, Oh Oh, Oops, and Swoops, were used to portray Hedwig in the motion picture *Harry Potter and the Sorcerer's Stone*.

The late Sterling Holloway, best known as the voice of Winnie the Pooh, was also the voice behind the "Give a hoot, don't pollute!" message of Woodsy Owl.

Paint

Early American farmers painted their barns with homemade paint made from a combination of milk, lime, linseed oil, and iron oxide (which gave it the familiar rusty-red color). The long-wearing but inexpensive mixture protected the barn from weather.

Due to the wide variety of chemicals used in its production, leftover or unused paint is considered hazardous household waste and should *not* be discarded with regular trash.

The use of lead paint in residential structures was banned in the United States in 1978, but homes built prior to that time may still contain the dangerous paint. Studies show that even very low levels of lead can cause brain and kidney damage in children.

Michael E. Brady, the model for the Dutch Boy Paint icon, wasn't from the Netherlands. He was an Irish-American who happened to live near the artist who created the logo.

Various forms of paint have been around since prehistory, but it wasn't until the nineteenth century that folks used the stuff to decorate and protect their homes. Prior to that, paint was mainly used for making signs.

When Henry Sherwin first offered ready-mix paint to the marketplace, the only color available was "raw umber in oil."

Harley Warrick was a professional painter for 45 years. His only job was to paint advertisements for Mail Pouch Tobacco on the sides of barns, which he did more than 20,000 times across 25 states.

Paintings & Painters

Many famous painters became known solely by their last names, but not Rembrandt, who was born Rembrandt Harmenszoon van Rijn.

Leonardo da Vinci's *Mona Lisa* has no eyebrows; it was the fashion at the time for women to shave them.

Archibald Willard's famed *Spirit of '76* painting, depicting a trio of weary colonial marchers (with flag, fife and drum), was painted in 1876, not 1776.

The persons depicted in Grant Wood's *American Gothic* aren't intended to be husband and wife, but father and daughter.

Then-wife Christie Brinkley painted the image used on the cover of Billy Joel's 1993 album *River of Dreams*.

Commenting on the over-the-top preparations often made by locations expecting her visit, Princess Diana once remarked "Everywhere I go, I smell fresh paint."

Pencils

While you can't get lead poisoning from pencils since they're made of graphite, graphite dust can lead to diseases of the lungs.

A typical pencil could draw a straight line estimated at 35 miles in length.

Today's pencil leads are usually made from graphite-and-clay paste that has been formed into rods. The leads become hard after being heated in an oven to about 1800°F.

Cedar trees are the variety most commonly used to make pencils. In fact, early pencils were sold unpainted to showcase the quality of the wood from which they were crafted.

While pencils with erasers are common in America, they're rarer in Europe. The theory is that the convenience of a built-in eraser makes it easier to make mistakes.

The crimped metal "collar" that holds the eraser to a pencil is called a *ferrule*.

Originally round, modern pencils are produced in a hexagonal shape since they're comfortable to hold and don't roll off tables as easily. As an added benefit, less wood is wasted.

The Pentagon

The Pentagon was designed so that no part of the structure was more than seven minutes' walk from any other part.

Made up of five pentagonal "wedges" connected by five pairs of corridors, the Pentagon building is five stories tall, and the interior court is five acres in size.

Completed in 1943, the Pentagon cost $50 million to build. Repairs following the 9/11 terrorist attack on the structure amounted to $700 million.

The Pentagon has six different ZIP codes, one for each section: Army, Navy, Marines, Air Force, Joint Staff, and Secretary of Defense.

Had the Pentagon not been built during wartime, when metal was being conserved for other uses, the structure would have been constructed with steel beams instead of concrete ones.

The Pentagon has about three times as much floor space as the Empire State Building.

The central plaza in the middle of the Pentagon is the largest "no-salute" area anywhere in the world. Military salute protocol does not apply there.

Pet Food

Cats cannot survive on dog food because of the different blend of nutrients. Our feline friends require five times as much protein as dogs do.

The German Shepherd on labels of Strongheart dog food was a bone-a-fide Hollywood celebrity, the subject of two books, and credited with appearing in five films.

Fish who feed off the water's surface can develop swim bladder disorder. To prevent this, soak the food flakes before adding them to the water so that they will sink.

In large quantities, chocolate, onions, grapes, and raisins can be poisonous to dogs.

Purina's long line of pet foods includes Rabbit Chow, Bird Chow, Guinea Pig Chow, and Monkey Chow.

The original Morris the Cat was a 15-lb. orange tabby named Lucky, rescued from an Illinois animal shelter only hours before he was scheduled to be put to sleep.

Don't feed avocado to your feathered friends; the fruit is poisonous to nearly every species of bird.

Phrase Origins

"Mad as a hatter" is thought to have derived from the fact that the nervous systems of haberdashers of old were affected by the mercury used to make felt hats.

The *Felix the Cat* TV show popularized the use of the name Poindexter as a generic term for "egghead."

As a horse ages, its gums recede; one that is old is literally "long in the tooth," which is how that phrase got its meaning.

The area containing the cheap seats in vaudeville theaters came to be known as the "peanut gallery," since patrons there unhappy with the show would sometimes pelt the act with empty shells.

English speakers adopted the phrase "pardon my French" after it appeared in *Harper's* magazine in 1895. It referenced the fact that culture in France was more permissive and even risqué.

"Pleased as Punch" refers back to the Punch & Judy puppet acts, most of which ended with Punch victorious (and smiling).

Pickles

According to Pickle Packers International, a perfect whole pickle has an average of seven "warts" per square inch.

Amerigo Vespucci, the explorer for whom most historians believe our country is named, was also a pickle merchant.

In pickle lingo, "kosher" has nothing to do with the Jewish faith. It simply means that garlic has been added to the brine mix. Plain dill pickles contain no garlic.

Pickling cucumbers are different from the long, smooth cukes we use in our salads (which are called "slicers" by those in the industry).

Cleopatra believed that eating pickles enhanced her beauty. Of course, historians now believe that her beauty was more fiction than fact.

When Hall of Fame baseball pitcher Nolan Ryan's hands developed blisters (a common ailment amongst hurlers), he reportedly soaked them in pickle brine.

The phrase "in a pickle" is thought to have been coined by William Shakespeare, who used it in his play *The Tempest.*

Pigeons

A carrier pigeon named Gustav, employed by the Reuters news service, was the first to deliver to Britain news of the Allies' landing at Normandy. He covered 150 miles to Portsmouth in only 5 hours.

On earlier pinball machines, the "tilt" mechanism was known as the "stool pigeon."

To help absorb the shock from its pecking at food on hard surfaces, a pigeon's beak is softer at its base than at the tip.

In 1810, an ornithologist named Alexander Wilson reported seeing a passenger pigeon flock 250 miles in length (and containing perhaps two billion birds) in the sky over Kentucky. Just over a century later the species was extinct.

While Big Bird was the most popular bird on *Sesame Street*, uptight Bert had a fondness for a different species: his pet pigeon, Eunice.

They're occasionally confused because of their similar styles, but it was Tom Lehrer, not Allan Sherman, who scored a novelty hit with "Poisoning Pigeons in the Park."

Doves and pigeons are so closely related that some etymologists make no distinction between the two.

Postage Stamps

The first self-adhesive stamp in the United States was a special "Peace on Earth" holiday issue from 1974. The glue didn't stick, and the experiment was deemed a failure. (It was another 18 years before self-adhesive stamps became the norm.)

It was difficult to distinguish the cancellation marks on Britain's first stamps, the "Penny Blacks." Later editions were printed in other colors to solve the problem.

From 1998 to 2000, the USPS issued a "Celebrate the Century" stamp series featuring twentieth-century icons, everything from Superman and the Slinky to *Seinfeld* and *Star Trek*.

In the early 1970s, the nation of Bhutan issued a series of postage stamps that actually doubled as phonograph records (which included both spoken language and music).

The USPS's Breast Cancer Research stamp, a "semipostal" issue for which a percentage of the purchase price goes to charity, has raised more than $50 million since 1998.

You can have a letter postmarked anywhere in the country by placing proper postage on it and sending it (inside a larger envelope) to the postmaster of the city of choice.

Great Britain's stamps are the only ones in the world not to have the country's name printed on them. In 1840, they became the first nation to issue postage stamps.

Potpourri

The first locomotive whistle was devised by George Whistler, whose son James became a celebrated American painter. Other whistles were around long before the invention, however, so the Whistler name is just a coincidence.

The first Bibles printed in the Western Hemisphere were published in 1661 in the language of the Algonquin Indians.

While Edmund Halley was smart enough to accurately predict the return of the comet bearing his name, he was dense enough to believe that the Earth was hollow on the inside.

If you can't identify whether a refrigerated egg is raw or boiled, try spinning it on a flat surface. If it spins freely, it's hard-boiled; otherwise, it's still raw.

The male and female of certain species of penguins are so similar that even experts have difficulty telling them apart.

Tennis players may get tennis elbow, tennis knee, and even *tennis breast*. Female players tend to "develop" more on their favored side (right-handed or left-handed).

Kazakhstan isn't one of those tiny "splinter" republics from the former USSR; in fact, the nation covers an area about four times the size of Texas.

Presidents

The first president to throw the first pitch at a Major League Baseball game was William Howard Taft. The first to do so as a southpaw (left-handed) was Harry S. Truman.

By law, a person has to be 35 years of age, a natural-born U.S. citizen, and a resident of the United States for at least 14 years to be eligible to run for president.

More U.S. presidents have been Episcopalian than any other religious denomination, followed by Presbyterian.

Weather and work permitting, President John Quincy Adams enjoyed taking a nude dip in the Potomac River once a day.

The resignation of Richard Nixon in 1974 meant that, for two years, the United States was governed by a president and vice-president neither of whom had been voted into office.

Jimmy Carter, who took office in 1977, is actually four months *younger* than George H. W. Bush, who left the presidency in 1993.

While John Adams, Thomas Jefferson, and James Monroe all died on July 4, only one president was born on that date: Calvin Coolidge.

Elvis Presley

The tune for Elvis's hit "Love Me Tender" came from a pre-Civil War song titled "Aura Lee."

Elvis Presley's hair was naturally light brown; he dyed it black to match Tony Curtis, whose "look" he wanted to emulate.

Daughter Lisa Marie Presley was born to Elvis and wife Priscilla on February 1, 1968, exactly nine months after the couple's marriage on May 1, 1967.

It didn't take long to turn Elvis-the-singer into Elvis-the-film-star. His first movie, *Love Me Tender,* opened only eight months after the release of his first album.

As a radio announcer, future game show host Wink Martindale met Elvis Presley, and the two developed a lifelong friendship.

Elvis' middle name is spelled incorrectly on his tombstone; it's shown as "Aaron" when his birth certificate specifies "Aron."

Elvis played racquetball shortly before he died, but unlike most of us, he didn't have to leave his property to do so: Graceland's backyard houses its own racquetball court.

Prisons

Robert Stroud, known as the Birdman of Alcatraz, only kept birds when he was serving time at Leavenworth. He had none when he was moved to Alcatraz, as they weren't allowed.

Around two million Americans are currently detained in jails and prisons across the country. No other nation has as many incarcerated persons.

In order to avoid affiliation with the Sing Sing prison, the New York town that was home to the facility changed its name in 1901 to Ossining (a different name for the same Native American tribe that originally claimed the land).

The 1971 riot at Attica State Prison was due to more than overcrowding. The convicts claimed they were only allowed one shower and one small roll of toilet paper each week.

David Marshall Williams spent much of his time in Caledonia State Prison repairing and designing firearms at the facility's machine shop. His invention of the short-stroke piston for the M-1 Carbine gave America a key advantage during World War II.

An estimated 6 in 10 federal prison inmates were placed there after being convicted of one or more drug offenses.

About three in four murder cases reported in the United States results in an arrest, and about three in four of these result in a conviction.

Dr. Samuel Mudd, jailed for conspiracy after setting assassin John Wilkes Booth's broken leg, was sent to a Key West prison. He was pardoned four years later after attending to both prisoners and guards during a yellow fever epidemic.

Radio

Over the last 20 years, while the number of AM stations in the United States has remained stable, the number of FM stations has nearly doubled.

Two of radio's best-known names, Rush Limbaugh and Howard Stern, share more than a media. They also share a birthday: January twelfth.

While there are exceptions, the Mississippi River is the approximate dividing line between stations with "K" call letters (to the west) and "W" ones (to the east).

It's no wonder that late disc jockey Wolfman Jack adopted such a wild personality. Had he used his birth name, he'd have become known by the rather generic Bob Smith.

Radio reaches more persons over the age of 12 on a weekly basis than any other media form; more than 95 percent of adults listen to the radio at least once a week.

As of 2006, the United States was home to five folk music radio stations, six that play nothing but bluegrass, and 11 dedicated to the blues. The top format was country, with more than 2,000 stations nationally.

While most recordings were still made in monaural only at the time, the FCC first authorized stereo FM broadcasts in 1961.

Reality TV

One of the first "reality" series was a 1973 PBS 12-part documentary called *An American Family.* Cameras chronicled the Loud family of Santa Barbara, California, including son Lance's "coming out" and wife Pat's demand for a divorce.

Richard Hatch, the first winner of CBS's *Survivor,* pled guilty to two counts of tax evasion in 2005. He forgot to claim his $1 million winnings ... but the IRS didn't forget him.

The subjects of the first season of *Bridezillas* were originally told that they were being filmed for a series about upscale New York weddings, and were unaware that the end product would focus on their tantrums and stressed-out behavior.

Apprentice contestant Sam Solovey locked his place on the show by paying someone at the front of the audition line $50 to let him cut in, then bragging about it at his initial interview.

Today's reality show contestants are typically screened by at least two psychologists before making the cut, a practice begun after a contestant from the Swedish show *Expedition Robinson* stepped in front of a train after getting the boot.

To find suitable subjects for *Nanny 911*, casting directors Debbie and Lisa Ganz prowl toy stores and Wal-Mart stores looking for mothers with screaming, uncontrollable children.

Even though Fox billed him as a $19,000-per-year construction worker, *Joe Millionaire* star Evan Marriott had previously earned some extra cash by modeling revealing swimwear and undergarments for California Muscle.

Red

In Muslim nations, the Red Cross is known as the Red Crescent.

Only once did the Reds and Red Sox meet in the World Series—in 1975, when Cincinnati won the matchup four games to three.

Concerned that customers might think it contained a red dye that the FDA had banned, the makers of M&M's took red candies out of the mixture in 1976. They were reintroduced nine years later.

In the mid-1940s, two ruddy-haired men worked as dishwashers in the same NYC eatery. Nicknamed Chicago Red and Detroit Red, the two came to be known (respectively) as Redd Foxx and Malcolm X.

In 1988, Maine became the first U.S. state to issue a license plate depicting a dead creature. The lobster on the plates was red, a color they only turn when they're being cooked.

The term "red-letter day" goes back to the centuries-old custom of using red ink to indicate holy days on the calendar.

Even though the name of the Indian Red crayon didn't refer to Native Americans, Crayola changed its name to Chestnut to avoid any confusion.

"Pink" became a color thanks to light red carnations, whose flowered edges are serrated ("pinked").

Redundant Abbreviations

Some abbreviations and acronyms are commonly used in a redundant fashion, such as "ATM machine." Since "ATM" means "Automatic Teller Machine," using the word "machine" again is pointless. Here's a short list of some other examples:

- ABS system (Automatic Braking System)
- DC current (Direct Current)
- HIV virus (Human Immunodeficiency Virus)
- LCD display (Liquid Crystal Display)
- MFP fluoride (Maximum Fluoride Protection)
- OPEC countries (Organization of Oil-Producing Countries)
- PIN number (Personal Identification Number)

- SAT test (Scholastic Assessment Test)
- UPC code (Universal Product Code)

Reptiles

The chameleon can extend its tongue one and one-half times the length of its body.

Alabama's waterways were once home to so many small reptiles that it became known as "The Lizard State."

A two-headed turtle found in Minnesota was displayed at the Minnesota Museum of Science, where it died in 1977 (on July 7 and July 8).

The creature appearing on the Izod logo is a crocodile, not an alligator (as commonly thought).

The Galapagos turtle can weigh 550 lbs., but that's tiny compared to the extinct *Stupendemys geographicus* turtle, which may have topped 2.5 tons.

Each year, an estimated 90,000 humans become infected with salmonella from reptiles kept as pets.

Frasier star Kelsey Grammer provided the voice of the gecko in the earliest Geico commercials featuring the lizard, back in 1999.

Snapping turtles love the taste of rotting flesh, so in the past, they were tethered and used to help find the corpses of drowning victims.

Resignations

Long before he hosted *Who Wants to Be a Millionaire*, Regis Philbin played second fiddle to Joey Bishop on a 1960s late-night talk show. Reege tearfully announced during a live broadcast that he was tired of Bishop's wisecracks and walked off the set.

During the recording of the "White Album," Beatle Ringo Starr became fed up with the in-fighting among the band, and was miffed that Paul McCartney played drums on several tracks. He quit the band in August 1968 but was lured back after a few weeks.

When McLean Stevenson informed the producers of TV's *M*A*S*H* that he'd signed a contract with a rival network, they responded by killing his character in a plane crash, both for dramatic effect and to ensure that Stevenson could never return to the show.

Geri Halliwell (Ginger Spice) was already weary of the constant touring and lack of free time, but the final straw that caused her to quit The Spice Girls was when their management refused to allow her to participate in a breast cancer documentary.

Esther Rolle quit the sitcom *Good Times* in 1977 after Jimmie Walker became a breakout star. She felt that the scheming, stereotypical character of J. J. Evans set a bad example for black youth.

John C. Calhoun was the first Vice President of the United States to resign his office, and he did so to move *down* the political ranks. He quit in 1832 to take a seat in the Senate, where he felt he would have a more effective role.

The only other vice president to resign the office did so in 1973 after pleading "no contest" to charges of tax evasion. His name was Theodore Spiros Anagnostopoulos, better known as Spiro Agnew.

Roadways (Big & Small)

Major U.S. Interstate numbers generally follow a pattern: odd-numbered ones run north and south, while even-numbered ones travel east and west.

Four-foot-wide Fan Tan Alley in Victoria, British Columbia, Canada, is thought to be the narrowest street in North America.

In 1952, the first motel in the Holiday Inn chain opened on U.S. Highway 70 in Memphis, Tennessee.

Mapmakers often add a nonexistent street (with a fake name) to city maps in order to prevent others from illegally reproducing them. If another publisher's map features the same street, copyright infringement can be proven.

Sesame Street is certainly one of America's most famous thoroughfares. If you're looking for Big Bird's nest, the address number is 123½.

Not every Interstate highway connects two or more states. By definition, an Interstate highway is a roadway that has been constructed under the auspices of the part of the Eisenhower Interstate Highway System.

The color of the center stripe on a roadway is an indicator of the direction of traffic. White lines mean both lanes run the same direction, while yellow lines indicate a division between two opposite traffic lanes.

Sandwiches

Before they became unified under the name Hawaii, the archipelago was known as the Sandwich Islands.

In diner lingo, certain sandwiches have their own names. A grilled cheese is known as a *jack*, while a ham sandwich is a *pig between sheets*.

Per a 2005 poll sponsored by Smucker's, nearly 60 percent of America's youth have at least one peanut butter and jelly sandwich each month.

Usually served on pita bread, the gyro sandwich is based on the Greek word for "circle," since the slab of lamb from which the meat is sliced is typically broiled on a rotating spit.

While the concept had been around for centuries, the "sandwich" got its name in 1762, after John Montagu (the Earl of Sandwich) popularized it as a way to snack while not interrupting his gambling activities.

The sandwich came into its own in 1930, when Continental Baking introduced the first pre-packaged sliced bread, Wonder Bread.

Lunch is the time for sandwiches. About half of all sandwiches consumed by Americans are eaten at lunchtime.

Santa Claus

Per the last several editions of the *Forbes Fictional 15*, Santa Claus is the world's richest fictional character, with a net worth of $∞ (infinity).

In 1962, the cover of *Esquire* featured an image of African-American boxer Sonny Liston in a Santa hat. More than one dozen advertisers, upset with the photograph, cancelled their contracts with the magazine.

Certain U.S. post offices are popular for holiday postmarks. One of the most popular is Santa Claus, Georgia, a small town of only about 250 residents.

Shirley Temple once admitted that she stopped believing in Santa Claus when she was six years of age, after she met him in a department store and he asked her for her autograph.

A 2001 study of Santa's "shopping mall" helpers confirmed what kids had known for years: the big guy's favorite snack is chocolate chip cookies and milk.

Three things you may not know about "'Twas the Night Before Christmas":

- The name "Santa Claus" is not mentioned anywhere in the text.

- When first published in 1823, the list of reindeer ended with Dunder and Blixem, not Donner and Blitzen.

- The poem's proper title is "A Visit from Saint Nicholas."

Saturday Night Live

Many of the earliest *Saturday Night Live* episodes had multiple guest stars. The premiere episode, for instance, featured both Janis Ian (who performed the show's first song, "At Seventeen") and Billy Preston.

Saturday Night Live was developed in 1975 after Johnny Carson requested that the network stop airing *The Best of Carson* on weekends.

Due to the nature of the hosts involved, *Saturday Night Live* was twice broadcast using a seven-second delay: In 1975, when Richard Pryor appeared, and again for Andrew 'Dice' Clay in 1990.

Despite common belief that he was a cast member, Steve Martin was never a regular on *Saturday Night Live*. He has, however, hosted the show more than a dozen times.

The show was known only as *Saturday Night* at first, to avoid confusion with an existing ABC variety show titled *Saturday Night Live with Howard Cosell*.

The youngest host of *Saturday Night Live* was Drew Barrymore, who appeared on the show in 1982 at only seven-and-a-half years of age.

 During the show's first season, Chevy Chase said "Live, from New York, it's Saturday Night!" in all but two shows. Garrett Morris spoke the line on one episode, and then-President Gerald Ford on the other.

Scandinavia

The list of nations that comprise Scandinavia include Denmark, Norway, and Sweden. From there, sources differ, but most include Iceland (and sometimes Finland) as well.

There's a 95 percent chance that anyone you happen to meet who comes from Denmark will be a member of the Lutheran religion.

In the late 1970s, one organization rivaled Volvo as the top-selling export to come out of Sweden. This group was better known as the pop vocal band ABBA.

Reykjavik, Iceland, is located farther north than any other national capital on Earth.

Will you have to go to Sweden or Norway to pick up your Nobel Prize? It depends. It's the latter if you won the Peace Prize, the former if you won for another field.

Is the proper term Norse or Norwegian? As adjectives, "Norse" is most often used when referring to the medieval era, while "Norwegian" concerns modern Norway.

Minnesota, the land of 10,000 lakes, has nothing on Finland, which is estimated to have six times as many.

Schools

It's not tough to figure out where Michigan State University or the University of Southern California are located. Other school names may not be as easy to place on a map, however. Here's a list of select examples:

Auburn, Troy State	Alabama
Loyola Marymount, Pepperdine, Stanford	California
Fairfield, Trinity, Yale	Connecticut
George Washington, Georgetown, Howard	District of Columbia
Bethune-Cookman, Stetson	Florida

Emory, Mercer, Morehouse	Georgia
Bradley, DePaul, Northwestern	Illinois
Ball State, Butler, Purdue, Notre Dame	Indiana
Drake, St. Ambrose	Iowa
Grambling State, Tulane	Louisiana
Bowie State, Johns Hopkins	Maryland
Holy Cross, Harvard, Northeastern	Massachusetts
Ferris State, Kettering, Wayne State	Michigan
Princeton, Rutgers, Seton Hall	New Jersey
Colgate, Cornell, Vassar	New York
Duke, Wake Forest	North Carolina
Kent State, Xavier	Ohio
Langston, Oral Roberts	Oklahoma
Bucknell, Lehigh, Temple, Villanova	Pennsylvania
Brown, Roger Williams	Rhode Island
Clemson, Furman, Winthrop	South Carolina
Austin Peay State, Vanderbilt	Tennessee

Baylor, Rice, Southern Methodist	Texas
William & Mary, James Madison	Virginia
Marshall, Mountain State	West Virginia
Lawrence, Marquette	Wisconsin

Shakespeare

William Shakespeare was forced to wed Anne Hathaway, eight years his senior, after she turned up pregnant.

The first "knock-knock" joke appears in the text of Shakespeare's *Macbeth*.

Among the many words that Shakespeare has been credited with coining are *critic, vulnerable, lonely, dwindle, bedroom*, and *exposure*.

Shakespeare was born in 1564, the same year that Michelangelo passed away.

The exact spelling of William Shakespeare's last name is a matter of conjecture; family records vary the spelling greatly, and the few existing copies of his signature don't even match.

In 1964, to honor the 400th anniversary of his death, Shakespeare became the first British "commoner" to appear on an official U.K. postage stamp.

Sharks

Great White Sharks must constantly swim at a speed in excess of 2 mph in order to get enough oxygen to survive.

In 1995, Americans purchased $50 million worth of shark cartilage in response to its reported anti-cancer properties (which were later proven to be false).

Grey Nurse Sharks are cannibals even before they're born. The young grow jaws and teeth while still in the uterus, and sometimes devour each other inside the womb.

The film *Jaws* owed much of its success to television. The studio spent nearly $750,000 to run trailers for the movie on national TV, the first time the tube had been widely used to promote a motion picture.

Dried-out sharkskin is so rough that it was once commonly used as sandpaper.

While Florida has been the location of about 60 percent of the reported shark attacks on U.S. beaches, more *fatal* shark attacks have occurred off the coast of Hawaii.

Three times as many reported shark attacks have occurred on the Pacific coast of North America than anywhere else in the world.

While most shark attacks come from just below the surface (and occur in shallow water), the sign of a shark's fin above the water is not a sign of aggression.

Shopping & Retail

The first Wal-Mart, Kmart, and Target stores all opened in the very same year: 1962.

In 1939, the U.S. Thanksgiving holiday was moved from the last Thursday in November to the fourth Thursday in November to extend the holiday shopping season for retailers.

Contrary to popular belief, the day after Thanksgiving is not the biggest shopping day of the year. Typically, it's the last Saturday before Christmas.

The Apple I computer system was introduced in 1976 for the devilish price of $666.

If the estimated one million Americans who make their living on eBay were employees, it would be the nation's third-largest employer, behind only McDonald's and Wal-Mart.

Introduced during the Great Depression, Ritz crackers were given their high-class name to inspire buyers (even though they sold for only 19 cents a package).

While it's not widely known, all items purchased online are subject to a state "use tax," which the buyer is legally obligated to include in the details of his state income tax return.

Silver & Gold

The first "gold rush" in America occurred in the mountains of northern Georgia in 1829, nearly 20 years before the precious metal was discovered in California.

Historians estimate that about 150,000 tons of gold have been mined in known history.

Any coin 10-cents or higher and dated 1964 and prior is worth more than its face value in metal, even if it's in too poor shape to be considered a collectible.

To be awarded an RIAA gold record in the United States, an album has to sell half a million copies. The U.K. equivalent is offered by BPI; gold albums there need only turn 100,000 units.

Gold purity is based on 24 karats total, meaning that 18-karat gold is three-quarters pure, while 14-karat is a bit more than half pure.

In U.S. Army insignia, silver is valued above gold in the ranks. For example, a lieutenant colonel (indicated by a silver oak leaf) outranks a major (with a gold oak leaf).

The Simpsons

The Simpsons has received at least one Emmy nomination every year since it first became eligible for the award in 1990.

Nancy Cartwright auditioned for *The Simpsons* in hopes of providing the voice for daughter Lisa. Instead, she was chosen to portray young Bart.

Sideshow Bob's prison number on *The Simpsons* was 24601, the same as Jean Valjean in Victor Hugo's *Les Misérables*.

On one episode of *The Simpsons*, neighbor Ned Flanders opened a "Leftorium" for Springfield southpaws. Not surprisingly, Simpson's creator Matt Groening is left-handed.

While he's known as Seymour Skinner, the man who is principal of Springfield Elementary on *The Simpsons* is actually an imposter named Armand Tamzarian.

Perpetually 10 years old, *The Simpsons Uncensored Family Album* reveals that Bart Simpson celebrates his birthday on April Fool's Day.

The late jazz saxophonist "Bleeding Gums" Murphy was revealed on an episode of *The Simpsons* to be the long-lost brother of Springfield physician Dr. Julius Hibbert.

Soap

Originally, Ivory soap was known simply as "The White Soap." The brand earned its new name when Harley Procter read the forty-fifth Psalm at church, describing an "ivory palace."

In eighteenth- and early nineteenth-century Britain, soap was widely available. It was so highly taxed, however, that only wealthy families could afford it.

Introduced in 1948, Dial soap owed its scent to 14 different oils and its deodorizing ability to *hexachlorophene*, a bacteria-killing powder discovered during World War II.

The first soap opera broadcast on an American television network was *Faraway Hill*, on the DuMont network, in 1946.

The role of Jodie Davis on *Soap* was comedian Billy Crystal's second appearance on a TV sitcom. His first was a guest spot on a 1976 episode of *All in the Family*.

Lever Brothers coined the term "B.O." (body odor) to give a name to the unpleasantness alleviated with their Lifebuoy brand of soap.

George Dawes Sr. developed a process to create "soap flakes," which he sold to Procter & Gamble in 1929 for only $500. Before his invention, laundry soap was only available in cake form.

Soft Drinks by the Numbers

4: The number of 16-ounce servings in a two-liter bottle of soda pop (with a little under four ounces left over).

7: The number of "natural flavors" purported in early advertisements for 7-Up, which is how the drink got its name.

20: The number of ounces in a typical bottle of soda pop in 2005. A standard-serving bottle from 50 years ago contained only half as much.

42: The number of different flavors of Faygo soda pop available as of 2006.

70: Years that the drink known as Dr Pepper included a period after the "Dr." The period was removed in 1955 to avoid confusion about the drink's purported medicinal properties.

72: The grams of caffeine in a 16-ounce serving of Pepsi One. This is 50 percent more than in the same amount of Pepsi or Diet Pepsi.

79: The number of days in 1985 that the original Coca-Cola was not produced by the company, in favor of "New Coke." The old recipe was reintroduced as "Coca-Cola Classic." (Coca-Cola didn't officially use "Coke" as an abbreviation of its brand name until the 1950s.)

Space

While Saturn's are far more spectacular visually, three other planets in the Solar System also sport rings: Jupiter, Neptune, and Uranus.

When you see the Sun from Earth, you're not seeing its current location, but where it was eight minutes ago. It takes that long for the light from the Sun to reach our eyes.

The first U.S. woman astronaut in space (Sally Ride) took to the stars some 20 years after the Soviet Union's first, Valentina Tereshkova in 1963.

The first married couple to travel together in space was Mark Lee and Jan Davis, who were members of the crew of *Endeavor* in 1992 for NASA's fiftieth space shuttle mission. (The two worked 12-hour shifts opposite one another.)

Since it was discovered in 1930, Pluto has moved less than one third of the way around the Sun in its estimated 248-year orbit.

While the Apollo 13 astronauts never made it to the Moon, they did set a record (which still holds as of 2006) for the human beings who traveled the farthest distance away from planet Earth.

Mercury and Venus are the only two planets in the solar system without a moon.

Sports Balls

If you've ever wondered why golf balls have all those dimples, here's the answer: studies have shown that they travel up to four times farther than smooth ones.

In the early days of football, an inflated pig's bladder encased in leather was used as the ball, hence the nickname "pigskin."

One of the trademarks of the American Basketball Association, which merged with the NBA 1976, was its distinctive red, white, and blue basketballs.

The WNBA now uses a similar orange-and-white version.

"Optical yellow" became the preferred color for tennis balls once the game was regularly televised (it showed up better on-camera).

Table tennis, or ping pong, balls are not hollow—they're filled with a small amount of pressurized gas, which prevents them from breaking too easily.

A regulation Major League baseball is held together with 108 stitches.

Indoor volleyballs are molded and have smooth seams. Outdoor volleyballs are stitched and weigh a bit more in order to compensate for the wind.

American football is played in the United States, Canadian football in Canada, and Australian Rules football in Australia and New Zealand. Elsewhere in the world, "football" is soccer.

Sports Jerseys

In 1998, every Major League Baseball team retired jersey #42 in honor of the player credited with breaking the sport's "color barrier," Jackie Robinson. (Players who already wore the number were allowed to keep using it.)

A professional hockey player wearing a #1 jersey is almost certainly a goalie; only a handful of non-goalies have used the number in the NHL.

The New York Yankees were one of the first MLB teams to adopt uniform numbers, but their jerseys are still missing a feature incorporated by nearly every other team: player names across the shoulders.

When Rick Barry signed with the NBA's Houston Rockets in 1978, he couldn't keep his favorite jersey number (24), as Moses Malone wore it. The future Hall-of-Famer came up with an ingenious solution: Barry wore #2 at home, while his road jersey depicted #4.

In the late 1970s, the Houston Astros wore colorful uniforms with the player numbers in a rather unusual place: on their pants (across the front left hip).

Unlike America's other major pro team sports (basketball, baseball and hockey), jersey numbers in the National Football League follow a particular pattern, as follows:

Jersey numbers	Position(s)
1 through 19	punter, kicker, quarterback
10 through 19	wide receiver*
20 through 49	running back, cornerback, safety
50 through 59	linebacker
60 through 79	offensive line
80 through 89	tight end, wide receiver*
90 through 99	defensive line

As many teams now carry extra wide receivers, they may now wear numbers 10 through 19 in addition to 80 through 89.

Star Wars

Of the 30 highest-grossing films in American history, *Star Wars* is the oldest movie on the list, first released in 1977.

Star Wars has received not one, but two series of facelifts since its original issue. The 1997 theatrical re-release incorporated many new elements, some of which were altered further for the 2004 video versions.

Unlike most films of its genre, *Star Wars* was a hit with the Academy as well as fans. The film won 6 of the 10 Oscars for which it was nominated.

In interviews, George Lucas has revealed that he seriously considered making *Star Wars* character Han Solo an alien rather than a human being.

Mark Hamill was involved in an automobile accident in late 1976 (shortly after *Star Wars* wrapped) which left him with a broken nose. Surgery was required to repair the damage done, and Hamill's different "look" has long been a topic of fans' interest.

In early drafts of the *Star Wars* script, Luke's last name was given as Starkiller instead of Skywalker.

The original *Star Wars* film earned the less-than-princely sum of just over $1.5 million in its opening weekend.

Stars & Galaxies

It's known as the Plough in Britain and the Casserole in France; in America, we call it the Big Dipper.

Proxima Centauri is the closest star to our solar system, but it's so dim that it cannot be seen with the naked eye.

Originally, the Milky Way wasn't the name of our galaxy, but the name of a much smaller belt of stars that form a whitish glow across Earth's sky at nighttime.

The "dog days" of summer are so-named because the period marks the time of year that Sirius (the Dog Star) is seen rising and setting with the Sun.

Although they appear close in the sky when viewed from Earth, stars in some constellations are actually thousands of light years away from one another.

Cosmonaut (meaning "space traveler") is a more accurate term for those humans who have gone into space than is *astronaut* (which means "star traveler").

About 5,000 years ago, the "North Star" was Thuban. Currently it's Polaris, and in about 12,000 years, Vega will take its place.

Stars Before They Were

Chuck Norris tried his hand at acting only after he was prompted to do so by one of his karate students, who happened to be an actor himself: Steve McQueen.

Until his comedy broke through, Jerry Seinfeld made his living various ways, notably as a light-bulb-selling telemarketer.

Sharon Stone was the winner of the spokes-model competition on the pilot episode of TV's *Star Search* back in 1983.

Prior to becoming a Hollywood star, Brad Pitt donned a chicken suit and appeared in promotions for the El Pollo Loco restaurant chain.

Before finding fame as a comic actress, Whoopi Goldberg was a desairologist (one who applies makeup to corpses for funerals).

As a youngster, Steven Spielberg discovered a novel (and profitable) money-making opportunity. He whitewashed the trunks of fruit trees in his neigh-borhood to repel pests.

Stars in World War II

Rod Serling, host and creator of the original *Twilight Zone* TV show, was awarded a Bronze Star for his efforts as an Army paratrooper during World War II.

Green Acres star Eddie Albert served in the U.S. Navy during World War II, taking part in several missions in the Pacific.

Jimmy Stewart wasn't just an actor; he was a Prince-ton graduate and a colonel in the Air Force. He continued to serve in the Air Force Reserves, eventually retiring as a brigadier general.

The first woman killed in the line of duty during World War II was Carole Lombard, whose plane crashed while she was on a war bond tour.

Later known as Marshal Matt Dillon on *Gunsmoke*, actor James Arness was awarded a Purple Heart after being wounded in action at Anzio.

The rough face that won Jack Palance an Oscar for *City Slickers* was in part because of reconstructive facial surgery he underwent after his bomber crash-landed in Britain in 1943.

Charles Durning couldn't seem to dodge the enemy during World War II; he was awarded not one, not two, but three Purple Hearts.

State Capitals

The names of the capitals of only four states begin with the same letter as the states themselves: Dover, Delaware; Honolulu, Hawaii; Indianapolis, Indiana; and Oklahoma City, Oklahoma.

Until 1873, the tiny state of Connecticut had two capitals: Hartford and New Haven.

Phoenix is the most populous state capital, and the only one home to more than one million residents.

When General William Sherman burned Atlanta in 1865, he didn't torch the governor's home.

That's because Georgia's capital at the time was 80 miles east in Milledgeville.

Honolulu, Hawaii, is closer to the equator than any other U.S. state capital.

Only four U.S. capital cities are named after presidents: Jackson, Mississippi; Jefferson City, Missouri; Lincoln, Nebraska; and Madison, Wisconsin.

State Flags

Only one U.S. state does not have a four-sided flag, and that's Ohio, which flies a five-sided "swallowtail" design.

Since 1900, seven different state flag designs have flown over the state of Georgia.

Except for the state seal in the center, the Florida state flag (with its red cross on a white field) is difficult to distinguish from the flag of neighboring Alabama.

Hawaii's flag is the only U.S. state flag to incorporate the British "Union Jack."

Half of America's state flags have a background of some shade of blue.

While the name Vermont literally means "green mountain" in French, the state's flag is blue. The only state with a green flag is Washington.

The moon can be seen on two state flags; most obviously on South Carolina's, and less conspicuously in the middle of the Missouri flag.

Supermarkets & Grocery Stores

Supermarkets quench your thirst more than they fill your stomach. The two top-selling item categories in a typical grocery store are carbonated drinks and milk.

If you think supermarkets gouge consumers, think again. The average after-tax profit pulled in by the stores over the last 25 years has been about 1 percent.

Piggly Wiggly was the home of two major grocery store innovations: it became the first self-service market in 1916, and the first shopping carts were used at the chain in 1937.

On a percentage basis, Americans spend about half as much of their disposable income on groceries as they did only 30 years ago.

The average supermarket carries between 40,000 and 50,000 items.

Arkansas is home to not only the nation's top-selling grocery retailer (Wal-Mart) but also the nation's top-selling food processor (Tyson).

Researchers are working on developing microchips that would allow supermarket items to interact with home appliances. A frozen dinner, for instance, could automatically "tell" a microwave oven the correct cooking time and temperature.

Symbol and Mark Names

´	acute accent
&	ampersand
˘	breve
ç	cedilla
^	circumflex accent
†	dagger
`	grave accent
∞	lemniscate
#	octothorpe
¶	pilcrow
~	tilde
/	virgule

Teeth

While you're looking your gift horse in the mouth, count its teeth. If it has 40, it's a male; if it has 36, it's a female.

Only about 1 in 2,000 babies is born with an exposed tooth.

Unless worn down by chewing, a rodent's teeth will grow continuously, rendering it unable to eat.

In Mexico, it's the Tooth Mouse, not the Tooth Fairy, that collects youngsters' teeth and leaves cash behind.

Popular Old West author Zane Grey wasn't a cowboy-turned-novelist. Before he moved to Arizona to write full-time, he worked in New York … as a dentist.

Sheryl Crow's wide smile isn't all hers; her front two teeth were knocked out when she slipped and fell during a concert early in her career.

Telephone

Despite inventing the telephone, Alexander Graham Bell never called his mother. He had a good reason, though; she was deaf.

Microbiological tests indicate that the receivers of public telephones are more germ-infested than the toilet seats in most public restrooms.

The first direct-dialed overseas call was placed in 1967; the U.S.-England conversation cost four dollars a minute.

Bell Laboratories introduced the Princess phone in 1959, but it wasn't until four years later that they managed to develop a ringer small enough to fit inside the unit.

In 1972, the FBI arrested a small group of criminals who had discovered a way to tap into free long distance service using a toy whistle found in boxes of Cap'n Crunch cereal.

The earliest pay telephones didn't have coin boxes; they were managed by attendants who accepted the money in person.

Tennis

Unlike most sports, tennis may be played on a variety of surfaces, including asphalt, clay, concrete, grass, or even wood.

The players taking part in the 650+ matches at Wimbledon each year exhaust a combined total of around 40,000 tennis balls during the two-week event.

Short pants weren't part of the tennis attire for men until about 1940.

The word "tennis" is based on the Old French word *tenez*, meaning "receive." The server shouted the word to warn his opponent that the ball was about to be put into play.

While lawn tennis is the game we all know and love, there's a less-common variety of the sport known as "court tennis," played indoors with a different rule set.

If the doctor diagnoses you with *lateral epicondylitis*, it might be time to hang up the racquet for a while. You're suffering from joint inflammation more commonly known as "tennis elbow."

Ken Rosewall holds two records at the Australian Open; he is both the youngest (at age 18 in 1953) and the oldest (at age 37 in 1972) to win the Men's Singles championship.

Thanksgiving Food

Besides wild turkey, the Pilgrims also enjoyed venison and seafood as entrées at the first Thanksgiving.

Green bean casserole, that staple of the Thanksgiving table, was created in 1955 by the folks at Campbell's Soup. The recipe has appeared for more than 50 years on cans of the company's condensed mushroom soup.

Turkey meat contains *tryptophan*, an amino acid that acts as a natural sedative, which adds to the "sleepy" feeling you get after enjoying a satisfying holiday meal.

When it comes to stuffing (or dressing), diners in the Midwest prefer a combination bread, celery, and onions, while New Englanders like to add oysters. Louisianans use andouille sausage, and people from Minnesota tend to prefer wild rice.

Even if they're called "yams," most American tables will feature sweet potatoes on Thanksgiving. True yams are rough, scaly tubers with dry, white flesh, and are native to Africa and Asia.

If you serve your dinner buffet-style, remember the two-hour rule: any food item sitting out at room temperature for two hours should be disposed of.

The Pilgrims didn't serve mashed potatoes at that first feast. Native to South America, potatoes were brought first to

Europe and then from there to North America
(where the first potato patch was planted in 1719).

The Theater

Broadway is the oldest major north-south thorough-
fare in New York City. It originated as a Native
American path known as Wickquasgeck Trail.

Playbill, generically used to refer to the program
distributed at a theater performance, is actually a
trademarked name.

Much to the chagrin of his father, Britain's Prince
Edward quit the Marines in 1987 to work in the
theater.

More lighted advertisements appear in the Times
Square/Broadway area than anywhere else in the
world, with the exception of Tokyo.

Americans currently purchase
more than 5.5 million Broadway
show tickets annually, with foreign visitors snapping up another
1 to 1.5 million.

The comedy term *slapstick* originated with traveling
Italian theater groups who would perform shows in
which characters would hit each other with wooden
noisemakers known by that name.

If you phone a box office for tickets on a particular
night only to be told that "the house is dark," it
doesn't mean that they forgot to pay their electric
bill, but simply that the show does not play on that
date.

Toilets

On an episode of TV's *Married ... with Children*, everyman-hero Al Bundy once constructed what he deemed the ultimate man's bathroom, with five rolls of toilet paper and no sink.

Per information gathered at the World Toilet Summit, the average person visits the "facilities" around 2,500 times annually.

The oft-repeated trivia chestnut about *Leave It to Beaver* being the first show on which a toilet was shown is a half-truth: only the tank of the toilet was seen on the episode.

Studies have shown that the stall closest to the door in a public restroom is typically the cleanest and least-used.

Old catalogues from department store retailers are rare, owing to several factors, including the use of the pages in the days before toilet paper became commonplace.

A short list of items Roto-Rooter has found lodged in plumbing fixtures over the years include sunglasses, keys, cell phones, photographs, nail clippers, and wallets.

A poll conducted by the folks at Scott indicated that persons aged 50 and older prefer to have their toilet paper dispensed over-the-top (by an amazing four-to-one ratio).

Tomatoes

When tomatoes were introduced to England from America, the plants were used only for decorative purposes, not as food, since it was commonly thought that tomatoes were poisonous.

Tomato juice is the main ingredient in V-8 Juice. The other seven vegetable juices in the mix are carrot, celery, beet, parsley, lettuce, watercress, and spinach.

Ketchup originated in China, where it was known as *ke-tsiap*, a fish sauce. Only after it spread to Europe did tomatoes become the mixture's base.

Botanists classify a tomato as a type of berry.

In appreciation of his innovative work involving their product, the folks from Campbell's Soup sent pop artist Andy Warhol two cases of their condensed tomato soup in 1964.

The first genetically altered food item to achieve FDA approval was the Flavr Savr tomato, in 1994.

The tomato is a member of the nightshade family, along with potatoes, eggplants, red peppers, and tobacco.

Trains & Railroads

When approaching a grade (traffic) crossing, you can identify an oncoming train by listening to the horn sequence: two long blasts, followed by one short and then one long.

Sheena Easton's first hit was released in Britain as "9 to 5," but to avoid confusion with Dolly Parton's hit of the same name, the U.S. title was changed to "Morning Train."

Through the Civil War, the rail gauge used in northern states was 4 feet 8.5 inches, making it incompatible with the 5-foot gauge commonly used in the south. After the war, the narrower of the two was made the national standard.

Only two months before his inauguration, Franklin Pierce and wife Jane were shattered when their only surviving child, 11-year-old Benjamin, was killed before their eyes in a train derailment accident.

Three of the railroads on the U.S. Monopoly board were based on real companies. The fourth, Short Line, is a bus service that still runs today between Atlantic City and New York.

The London Underground was opened in 1893. It is the oldest (and still the longest) subway train system anywhere in the world.

Completed in 1916, the Trans-Siberian Railroad stretches for 5,778 miles, a distance equivalent to a trip from New York to Los Angeles and back again.

The first Lionel electric model train set wasn't crafted as a toy, but as a display for a storefront window in New York City.

Trees

Oak trees don't produce acorns until they're at least 20 years of age, often older.

Lucky Charms cereal once offered green tree-shaped marshmallows as a promotion for Earth Day.

Maple trees in Europe can't be tapped for syrup; the colder weather there prevents the sap from forming properly.

With their flameproof bark, Redwood trees grow tallest after forest fires burn the other plants around them, giving them access to more nutrients in the soil.

It's the First Lady, not the U.S. President, who selects the theme for the White House Christmas tree decorations each holiday season.

Wood from evergreens should never be used in fires used for cooking; the soft wood can give off resins and tars that can harm the food.

Nearly half the forests in Haiti were lost in the decade from 1990 to 2000, leaving woods on only about 3 percent of the nation's total land area.

Trophies & Awards

You've probably heard of the trophy that was named for Frederick Arthur. He was also known as Lord

Stanley of Preston, and his trophy was (and still is) the Stanley Cup.

In its first year, the Academy of Television Arts & Sciences' award was called the Immy (for the *image orthicon tube*). Realizing that a more feminine name better suited the trophy, which depicts a woman, this evolved into Emmy.

Launched in 1959, the Grammy Awards were originally conceived to defend "quality" music against the onslaught of rock 'n' roll music. "Rock" wasn't added as a category in the ceremony until three years later.

The Major League Baseball pitcher to win the most games but never win the Cy Young Award was ... Cy Young.

In his role as newsman Lou Grant, actor Ed Asner became the first person to win two Emmy awards for the same character in two different series (*The Mary Tyler Moore Show* and *Lou Grant*).

The award money that accompanies the Nobel Prize varies year-by-year, depending on the amount of interest earned on the funds placed into the program (in recent years, the amount has exceeded $1 million U.S.).

Before he became a TV and film star, Will Smith became the first artist to win a Best Rap Performance Grammy when the category was first introduced in 1989.

Turkey Trivia

The loose skin hanging from the neck of a turkey is known as a wattle.

Normally, a turkey's wattle is a light blue or gray, but when excited or upset, it will turn bright red.

In bowling, the feat of throwing three consecutive strikes is called a *turkey*.

Native Americans hunted turkeys not only for meat, but for weaponry. The sharp spurs on the legs of toms (male turkeys) were used as arrowheads, and their feathers helped stabilize arrows in flight.

The city of Istanbul, Turkey, straddles two continents: Europe and Asia.

If you prefer the dark meat of turkey at Thanksgiving, it's best to ask for it early in the meal, since only 30 percent of the meat on a typical turkey is of that variety.

TV Freds

On *I Love Lucy*, Little Ricky named his dog Fred in hopes that the Ricardos' landlord and friend, Fred Mertz, would allow him to keep the dog in the family's apartment. Luckily, the scheme worked.

Fred Dalton Thompson is well known in Hollywood for roles in films like *Die Hard 2* and in several incarnations of TV's *Law & Order*, but he had quite a second career as well: that of a lawyer and U.S. senator from Tennessee.

The TV series *The Fugitive* was one of the medium's biggest hits during its era, following Dr. Richard Kimble's search for his wife's killer: a one-armed man named Fred Johnson.

Favorite animated Freds on television include Fred the Lion (assistant to *Super Chicken*), Fred Jones (head of the *Scooby Doo* gang), and, of course, Fred Flintstone.

Before he ended his life, *Chico and the Man* star Freddie Prinze Sr. was briefly engaged to the daughter of another famous comedian: Lenny Bruce.

Fred Grandy, who first came to fame as Gopher on TV's *Love Boat*, parlayed his popularity into a spot as a U.S. Congressman from his home state of Iowa.

McFeely was more than just the name of the Speedy Delivery agent on the children's TV show *Mister Rogers' Neighborhood*. It was also the middle name of the show's host, Fred Rogers.

Dancer Fred Berry portrayed the role of Freddie "Rerun" Stubbs on TV's *What's Happening!!* His nickname referred not to subsequent airings of the sitcom, but because he did poorly in school, causing him to have to repeat several classes.

TV Theme Songs

Mad About You star Paul Reiser not only co-wrote the show's theme song, but he also played piano on the tune.

As the studio wouldn't pay for singers, Vic Mizzy multi-tracked his own voice three times to create the "trio" that sang his theme song for *The Addams Family*.

The theme song for the decidedly British comedy *Monty Python's Flying Circus* is the decidedly American song "The Liberty Bell March," composed by John Philip Sousa.

Jerry Scoggins, who sang the vocals for *The Beverly Hillbillies* theme song, was a stockbroker by trade, and only sang part-time on weekends.

Only one TV sitcom's theme song hit #1 on the *Billboard* pop chart: John Sebastian's "Welcome Back," from the show *Welcome Back, Kotter*.

Carroll O'Connor and Jean Stapleton weren't originally approached to sing the *All in the Family* theme song. It only occurred as a cost-cutting measure after the series went over budget.

"Cleveland Rocks," one of the themes used for *The Drew Carey Show*, was a remake of an earlier tune titled "England Rocks," written and recorded by Ian Hunter in 1977.

Underwear

Boxer shorts were named due to their resemblance to the cut-off pants worn by pugilists. *Long Johns* got their name from a boxer, John L. Sullivan, who wore them in the ring instead of boxer shorts.

All-female pop band the Go-Go's performed an odd ritual during the band's early concerts: they coated underwear with bread crumbs and fried it onstage.

While Scarlett O'Hara made an issue of the dimensions of her waist, we'll never know what bra size she would have worn: the undergarments weren't developed (no pun intended) until 1914.

Elastic bands were originally sewn only into boxer shorts; early briefs didn't have them.

Hall-of-fame baseball pitcher Jim Palmer served as spokesman for Jockey underwear for nearly 20 years, earning more international fame than he did in his years in sports.

Colored undergarments were first developed during World War II, since standard white shorts and T-shirts proved too conspicuous on the battlefront when hung up to dry.

Brassieres were one-size-fits-all until Ida Rosenthal (founder of Maidenform) offered them in a selection of different "cup" sizes beginning in 1921.

Unusual Locations

The international airport serving Cincinnati is not in Ohio, but southwest of the city in Kentucky.

Since 1984, the New York Jets have played their home games in New Jersey.

The soft-rock trio known as America was perhaps more homesick than patriotic when they named the band. The group was formed in England by the sons of U.S. Air Force personnel stationed there.

A map showing longitude lines will confirm that the city of Los Angeles, California, is farther east than the city of Reno, Nevada.

The home of London Bridge isn't the British capital, but Lake Havasu City, Arizona. The structure was dismantled and shipped to America, where reconstruction was completed in 1971.

The most populous city in Missouri is Kansas City. (It has three times as many residents as Kansas City, Kansas.)

The first Kentucky Fried Chicken franchise was opened not in the Bluegrass State, but in the Beehive State, better known as Utah.

U.S. Census Facts

America's 10 most populous states account for more than half of the nation's total population.

For two decades, Nevada has annually led the nation in population growth. In fact, the state's population has more than doubled since 1990.

Alaska's population has nearly tripled since it was admitted to the Union in 1959. In the same time period, Nevada's population has increased nearly ten-fold.

Since 1920, North Dakota has experienced very little fluctuation in its population, holding steady in a range between 620,000 and 680,000.

In 1900, Missouri was America's fifth most populous state with over 3.1 million residents. A century later, it had dropped to seventeenth on the same list.

If Alaska (with the nation's lowest population density) had as many residents per square mile as New Jersey (with the highest), it would be home to more than 680 million persons.

Wyoming's population finally broke the half-million mark in 2003, making it the last of the 50 U.S. states to reach that plateau.

U.S. Coins & Currency

Zinc-coated steel pennies were minted by the United States during World War II to save copper. These are the only American coins that can be picked up using a magnet.

The tiny mint mark near the date on most U.S. coins indicates where it was minted. D represents Denver, P is for Philadelphia, and S means San Francisco.

The design of the Roosevelt dime has not changed since 1946, longer than any other current American coin.

Although the older ones are becoming rarer, you may still find three different types of $20 bills in your wallet. They were redesigned in 1996 and again in 2003.

You won't find a quarter dated 1975 in your pocket change. All the 25-cent pieces minted that year were of the special Bicentennial variety, marked with the dates 1776-1976.

Errors on the reverse of the 2004 Wisconsin entry in the "state quarter" series boosted those coins' values to nearly one hundred times their face value.

Abraham Lincoln's image appears on both sides of the penny; on the obverse in profile, and on the reverse as a tiny statue in the center of the image of the Lincoln Memorial.

The phrase "In God We Trust" began appearing on U.S. coins in 1864, but it wasn't adopted as our national motto until nearly a century later, in 1956.

U.S. States

Arkansas is the only U.S. state whose name begins with the letter "A" but does not end with "A."

Only one U.S. state borders three different Canadian provinces; Montana.

William Penn's writings indicate that he didn't wish for Pennsylvania to have his name; he wanted to call it New Wales.

Wyoming was the first U.S. state to allow women to vote.

A total of 17 U.S. states border a foreign nation. Four border Mexico, and the rest border Canada.

Because of the frigid weather that occasionally causes indoor plumbing to fail, Alaska is home to more outhouses than any other U.S. state.

Texas has more counties than any other state, with 259 of them. Second on the list is Georgia, with 159.

Valentine's Day

In the United States, more Valentine's Day cards are given to schoolteachers each year than to members of any other employment group.

There are at least three St. Valentines, and historians aren't certain which one inspired the current traditions.

Cupid was typically depicted as a handsome, virile young man until the Victorian Age, when he was "cleaned up" and changed into a cherubic little boy.

Wal-Mart founder Sam Walton wed Helen Robson on Valentine's Day in 1943. He passed away just a few months before the couple would have celebrated their 50th wedding anniversary.

Historians believe the long-used heart ♥ icon doesn't represent the human heart, but another part of the anatomy (most likely the female backside).

It's no wonder that most Valentine's Day cards are pink, since women purchase nearly 9 out of 10 of them.

Video Games

Way back in 1983, President Ronald Reagan was quoted as saying he believed that the video game age would result in a new generation of kids whose improved "hand, eye, and brain coordination" would help them become excellent military pilots.

There were reportedly more *E.T. the Extra-Terrestrial* game cartridges made in 1982 than there were Atari console systems to play them. Millions were returned (and destroyed).

In 1958, William Higinbotham at the Brookhaven National Laboratory developed what some consider to be the first video game, using a small analog computer and an oscilloscope. Similar to what became known as *Pong*, it was called *Tennis for Two*.

The name of video game manufacturer Coleco is an acronym of the brand's original name: the Connecticut Leather Company.

The 2001 "all your base are belong to us" Internet phenomenon was inspired by the video game *Zero Wing* and one of the more humorous Japanese-to-English mistranslations that appeared on one of its introductory screens.

In 1980, Midway smartly decided against adopting the suggested "Puck-Man" as the name for their new video game. The obvious potential for vandalism of the name led them to alter it slightly, to *Pac-Man*.

Unable to duplicate "real" music at the time, the 1982 arcade video game *Journey* (featuring the band of the same name) was fitted with a looping cassette that played the song "Separate Ways" during the game's bonus round.

Wacky Words

A short list of words that are only used in the plural form includes *binoculars*, *gallows*, *pliers*, and *trousers*.

"The five boxing wizards jump quickly" is an example of a *pangram*; a sentence that contains every letter of the alphabet at least once.

Hawaiians may have to worry about *aa*, but not so much about *oo*—aa is a rough flow of lava, while oo is a species of bird native to the islands.

Gunk is more than just a slang word for crud; it's a trademark for a degreaser made by the Solder Seal Company.

More words in the English language begin with "S" than any other letter of the alphabet.

The word *pedigree* comes from a phrase meaning "foot of the crane," due to the resemblance of the bird's three-toed foot to the lines drawn to represent family trees.

A few singular words not only become plural when you add an "s" to the end, but become singular again when another "s" is added. These include *bra*, *care*, and *prince*.

Monday is the only day of the week whose letters can be rearranged to form a word: *dynamo*.

The letters A, C, E, P, R, and S can be scrambled to make at least six different words: *capers*, *pacers*, *parsec*, *recaps*, *scrape*, and *spacer*.

No letter in the English language has two syllables. They each have one except for "W," which has three.

Water

Estimates reveal that as much as 25 percent of the bottled water sold in the United States is nothing but filtered "tap water."

The name "vodka" is based on a Russian word literally meaning "little water."

The cool moisture of cucumber slices, which are 90 percent water, help decrease swelling around the eyes by constricting the surrounding blood vessels.

South Dakota's Wall Drug Store found its niche in 1936 when owners installed their first "Free Ice Water" sign on a nearby roadway. The store has since formed its own community and has become one of the nation's most popular roadside attractions.

The fastest creature on land (the cheetah) still isn't as speedy as the fastest creature in water. The sailfish has been clocked swimming at speeds approaching 70 miles per hour.

Antifreeze should not be used full-strength. Undiluted, the fluid is less effective than when it's mixed with the prescribed amount of water.

More than 70 percent of the fresh water in U.S. homes ends up being used in the bathroom.

Weather

On August 10, 2003, something occurred in Britain that had not happened since records were first kept in 1870: the temperature reached triple-digits (100° Fahrenheit).

Only female names were given to hurricanes until 1991, when male names were added to the list. The first hurricane with a male name was Bob.

If you know a mountain's height, you can estimate the temperature at its peak; it drops 1.8°F for every 500 feet up.

Most tornadoes occur in North America, but Antarctica is the only continent where one has never been recorded.

The largest hurricane known to man isn't on Earth; it's Jupiter's "Great Red Spot," a huge storm three times Earth's size that has been raging on the planet's surface for centuries.

The island of Réunion in the Indian Ocean received an incredible 73.62 inches of rain in a single day on March 14, 1952.

The record high temperature ever measured in Alaska was 100°F. Surprisingly, that's exactly the same as the record high in Hawaii.

The White House

Since most of the groundskeeping staff had gone off to fight in World War I, Woodrow Wilson put sheep on the White House lawn to keep it trim. He even sold wool sheared from the sheep, donating the proceeds to the Red Cross.

The president and his family live on the second floor of the White House. The bedrooms for staff and guests are located on the third floor.

Among the accoutrements to keep the First Family entertained while on White House grounds are a bowling alley, a movie theater, a putting green, a tennis court, a jogging track, and a swimming pool.

Like most buildings of its era, the White House did not have indoor plumbing when initial construction was completed in 1800. That's right, even the president had to use an outhouse.

With certain food items rationed during World War II, FDR often complained about the bland menu served at the White House. Meal planner Henrietta Nesbitt had to regularly remind the president that he should set an example for the rest of the country.

Franklin Pierce, the fourteenth president of the United States, warmed up the White House winters in two important ways. His efforts resulted in both the first heating system and the first Christmas tree in the executive mansion.

The British captured and burned the White House during the War of 1812. The structure's outer stone walls remained standing, however, so it was possible for the interior to be completely rebuilt.

The Wizard of Oz

In L. Frank Baum's book *The Wonderful Wizard of Oz*, Dorothy was eight years of age. Judy Garland was 16 when she played the role in the movie.

The well-known quote is often altered and paraphrased when used in casual conversation, but

Dorothy's specific statement to her Cairn Terrier was: "Toto, I've a feeling we're not in Kansas anymore."

Ill and nearly blind in 1962, actress Clara Blandick, known to millions as Aunt Em in *The Wizard of Oz*, took her own life at the age of 82.

The "Haunted Forest" sign seen by Dorothy and her trio of friends is misspelled. The text points the way to the "Witches Castle" instead of "Witch's Castle."

At least three injuries delayed the making of the film:

- Buddy Ebsen, who had switched roles to play the Tin Man, had an allergic reaction to the aluminum makeup on his face, forcing producers to re-cast the role while he was hospitalized.

- Margaret Hamilton's copper makeup caught on fire during a scene in which her Wicked Witch of the West character "disappeared" in flames, resulting in burns to her arms and face.

- A palace guard accidentally stepped on Toto's foot, after which a "double" was brought in for two weeks while Terry (the dog's real name) was healing.

World History

Nero didn't fiddle about while Rome burned; for one thing, the violin wouldn't be invented for several hundred years.

Galileo's two daughters were sent at an early age to live in a convent (as was typical of girls of the era who were born out of wedlock).

Mesopotamia, once considered the cradle of civilization, is located in modern-day Iraq.

In his writings, explorer Marco Polo never mentioned tea drinking, foot-binding, or the use of chopsticks, leading many modern scholars to believe that he never really visited China.

The first British settlement in what is now Australia was a penal colony for criminals. It's now known as the city of Sydney.

Cape Horn was given its name in 1616, but not for the fact that it's shaped like a horn. Willem Schouten, the captain of the Dutch ship that explored the area, was born in the city of Hoorn.

Although Napoleon's men were said to have shot the nose away from the Great Sphinx, drawings of the wonder from the years leading up to his era show that the schnoz was already missing.

Yellow

The single largest Yellow Pages advertiser is U-Haul International.

The Beatles' speaking voices in the animated feature film *Yellow Submarine* were provided by actors.

While more than 40,000 persons in New Orleans died of yellow fever in the nineteenth century, the disease is now virtually nonexistent in the United States.

John Hertz, who gave his name to his own rental car company, was also the founder of the Yellow Cab Company.

The longest-titled #1 U.S. pop hit (not including parenthetical title information) is "Itsy Bitsy Teenie Weenie Yellow Polka Dot Bikini." Tied for second-longest is another "yellow" song, "Tie a Yellow Ribbon 'Round the Ole Oak Tree."

When fully ripe, limes are naturally yellow and are difficult to distinguish from lemons.

In the 1939 film *The Wizard of Oz*, the yellow brick road was shown spiraled around another road made of red bricks.

A four-year study published in 1995 indicated that yellow fire trucks were half as likely as red ones to become involved in traffic accidents at intersections.

Yiddish Phrases

Schmaltz, used to describe something that's ultra-sentimental or just plain gooey, comes from a German word that literally means "fat drippings."

Kibitz originates from a word that means "an onlooker at a game." Years ago, a kibitzer was a person who offered unwanted comments during a poker or chess game, but it has evolved to describe any unsolicited advice.

Maven, used to describe an expert or connoisseur, is actually a Yiddish word that comes from the Hebrew "meyvin," meaning "one who understands."

Chutzpah, roughly pronounced "hutz-pah," means gall or shamelessness. The classic example of chutzpah is the man who kills his parents and then asks the judge for leniency because he's an orphan.

The slang term "fin," meaning a five dollar bill, comes from the Yiddish word for "five," *finnif.*

Tuchus is the Yiddish word for the part of our body that goes over the fence last, and is the foundation for the more familiar word "tush."

Schnozz evolved from the Yiddish word "shnoitsl," which has its roots in the German word for "snout." Whatever the etymology, it made Jimmy Durante a star.

The Letter "Z"

The two Z-named women who won consecutive Best Supporting Actress Oscars in 2002 and 2003: Catherine Zeta-Jones and Renee Zellweger.

The first car in the famed Datsun Z-car lineup was called the Fairlady Z, named by company president Katsuji Kawamata who enjoyed a Broadway production of *My Fair Lady.* The car was later introduced to America as the 240-Z.

Two unrelated singers (from obviously different backgrounds) changed their real last names from Zimmerman before making it big: Bob Dylan and Ethel Merman.

The Ziegfeld Follies weren't shy to perform "trendy" shows. When pogo sticks took America by storm in the 1920s, choreographers developed a dance number incorporating the toys.

The real name of the nine-times-wed, Hungarian-born actress known as Zsa Zsa Gabor is Sari.

Introduced in 1920, the Zero candy bar is thought to have been named because the white fudge coating gave the treat a glossy, ice-like appearance, as in "zero degrees."

Both the nations of the world whose names begin with the letter "Z" are located on the continent of Africa: Zambia and Zimbabwe. (Zaire is now known as the Democratic Republic of the Congo.)